Access your Inner Power

Awakening Your Health and Vitality

Brenda Schnable

Copyright 2012 by Brenda Schnable
All Rights Reserved
Printed in the United States of America on acid-free paper

Illustrations by Krystal Watters
Book Design by Melinda Fine
Author Photograph by Marc Montocchio
Interior Photographs by Andrew Schnable

*To my family, Andrew, Kate, and Milli
with love and gratitude*

Contents

Part I
    Introduction
  1. Understanding Energy from A Western Perspective 7
  2. Understanding Energy from An Indian Ayurveda Perspective 9
  3. Understanding Energy from A Yoga Perspective 15
  4. Understanding Energy from A Qi Perspective 23

Part II
  5. What Is Health? 27
  6 What Is The Body 31
  7. Health, Vitality, and Healing The Western Way 39
  8. Health, Vitality, and Healing The Ayurveda Way 43
  9. Health, Vitality, and Healing The Yoga Way 53
  10. Health, Vitality, and Healing The Qigong Way 85

Part III
  11. Qi Infused Yoga 93

Part IV
  12. Qi Infused Yoga Practice 143
      Glossary 152
      End Notes 156

Part 1

Understanding your Inner Power

Introduction

Why I wrote this book - My Story

I'm Always Sick

All people have an experience in their life that stops them dead in their tracks and makes them reflect and take stock. Mine was in my late 20s. I was home sick from work. The phone rang, and I dragged myself to it.

"Hello," I answered in a barely audible voice.

"Oh," followed by a very pregnant pause, replied my boss in complete shock. I suddenly understood why he called; he didn't believe I was home sick again.

After that brief, awkward, and poignant conversation, I went back to bed, but not without a sense of unease. How could he believe I was not sick? I'm always sick. Ding, ding, ding! A light bulb went off – *I AM ALWAYS SICK*. By always, I mean always. As a child and teen, I was sick all the time. The difference then was youth was on my side, and I bounced back quickly. By my late twenties that was not the case.

For the next day or two, while lying in bed, I began to think about random things. Why am I always sick? Why do "old" people always say, "I have my health?" I thought about something Jack Lalanne, a pioneer in the fitness industry said "What good is it to be old if you can't walk, are taking all kinds of medications, can't go to the bathroom, or have satisfying intimate relations with your wife? What kind of quality of life is that?"

After I recovered, I made it my goal not to be sick. I decided to start an exercise routine. I bought several aerobic albums including the famously popular *Jane Fonda's Workout Record*. I exercised three to four times a week. I still got sick and could not live without having tissues with me at all times; however, I realized that I was getting sick less frequently. To me that was progress.

Hives

Then it happened, again. In 1990, after the birth of my second child, I couldn't exercise anymore. My body couldn't tolerate aerobics. I would break out in hives every time my body temperature rose. I was miserable physically, mentally, and emotionally. I was sick more often again. I gained weight (I was always one who gained weight easily) that I couldn't lose. After two years of misery, my doctor gave up and sent me to a dermatologist. After explaining the birth of my second child triggered the hives, her explanation was that my "internal thermostat" got turned up and never got turned back down. My feeling of elation finally having a diagnosis was short-lived as she explained the treatment—steroids. The steroids would not make the hives completely disappear, I would have mood swings (that was putting it mildly), and I would gain even more weight. This was not ideal but I was desperate so I took the steroids.

From the moment I left the dermatologists office, I realized I could not rely on doctors completely. I vowed I would figure this out myself. That was twenty years ago. I started my first yoga class shortly after that in June of 1992. That moment began my journey to regain my health.

Leukemia?

I was cruising on along. Making small, yet very impactful changes. I became a vegetarian. I quit my corporate job once and for all. I not only practiced yoga but also became a yoga instructor, then a yoga therapist. I was stronger and healthier. I could say I rarely got sick anymore and if I did, it didn't affect me has much. YAY! My journey to health was reaping rewards until…

On December 14, 2007 I distinctly remember looking at my ankle and noticing it was quite swollen. I thought, "What's causing that?" I went to the urgent care in February 2008, for other reasons, and asked the doctor to look at my ankle. He was dismissive and told me I twisted it without knowing it. I had a difficult time believing that I, a yoga instructor, would twist my ankle without knowing it.

Fast forward to the spring of 2010. I have been through all sorts of tests from all sorts of Western doctors. Nothing conclusive. I didn't fit into any of their silos, so "sorry, we can't help you." One doctor was a hematologist who I'd been seeing for about a year. He finally said I needed a bone marrow biopsy to determine what is going on with my blood and if I have leukemia. In the meantime, I talked to my friend, who is an energy worker. She gave me some proprietary exercises to do until my scheduled appointment for the biopsy.

The day came for the biopsy. They drew blood. And I waited. The doctor came in. He had to pick his jaw up off the floor. "What did you do in the last three weeks? Your blood is perfect!"

That's when I positively and absolutely knew without a doubt, I had the power to heal myself. My journey the last two years has been to understand that energy. And now, I share it with you.

Energy – A Path to Health

Ever since that wake-up call from my boss, I have studied Eastern and Western methods of fitness and health. What I discovered is while physical activity is great, it is just a piece of the puzzle. After years of doing aerobics and then yoga, I hit a ceiling. There was no question about it. I was definitely healthier but knew innately something was missing – I had to find the other pieces of the puzzle. I discovered one of the major pieces was energy.

Energy Systems

During my study of energy of the human body, I discovered many cultures have acknowledged and named the energy within the body—*Qi/Chi* (Chinese), *Prana* (India), *Mana* (Hawaiian), *Lüng*, (Tibetan Buddhist), *Ki*

(Japanese), and *Bioelectricity* (Western). The two main viewpoints focused in this book are the Western and the Eastern viewpoints. There are two major differences between the viewpoints: approach and tangibility.

The Western viewpoint is scientific, based on experiments and research. Once tangible evidence is found, the evidence is accepted as true. An example is the mitochondria. Discovered in the late 19th century, mitochondria convert energy used by the body's cell.

The Eastern viewpoint comes from observation. By observing how the body moves and reacts, complex energy systems were developed. The energy systems were accepted without experimentation and their results. That is, experiments were not developed to prove or disprove a theory nor were results needed before the energy systems were accepted as true.

Accessing Your Inner Power

When a piece of equipment, such as a cell phone or laptop, loses energy, it becomes less powerful, slower, and much less efficient. Your body and mind are the same. You operate and have your own energy. Your energy is your inner power. When your energy is strong, you are powerful. Conversely, when your energy is weak, you have no strength.

This book describes how the West and East view the human body and its energy. Explained in this book is how to access your inner power from both the perspectives. Beyond accessing your power is awakening your inner power. We all have energy and we can all access it. But like my former sickly self can attest, it was in a sleepy dormant state. It wasn't until I accessed and awakened my inner power, could my energy be utilized to the fullest for maintaining health, increasing vitality, and aid in healing.

After years of body work and self-discovery, I developed a unique practice, *Qi Infused Yoga* that is designed to work the energy systems while working the body instead of emphasis on just one or the other.

Qi Infused Yoga

Qi Infused Yoga accesses and awakens your inner power and focuses on the movement of energy. With Qi Infused Yoga, you exercise the body gently, awaken dormant energy, and get stagnant energy flowing. This fluid practice uniquely blends yoga poses with the movements of Qigong and Tai Chi. Qi Infused Yoga is perfect for beginners of any age. There are no intimidating yoga "pretzel" moves involved, and it is gentle on the joints. If standing is an issue, Qi Infused Yoga can also be practiced in a chair. Chapter 11 explains Qi Infused Yoga in depth and Chapter 12 provides three Qi Infused Yoga practices.

Chapter 1

Understanding Energy from a Western Perspective

Defining Energy

Energy is defined as the ability to do work. There are many types of energy; mechanical, solar, chemical, electrical, sound, thermal, and nuclear. All but solar and nuclear energy can be found in the body. Solar energy does, however, indirectly enter the body by the food we eat. Of these types, the most relevant are mechanical and electrical.

Kinetic and potential energy are the two types of mechanical energy. Kinetic energy is the energy of motion, whereas potential energy is stored energy. An example of kinetic energy is walking, scratching an itch, and blinking your eyes. Kinesiology is the study of human movement. It applies the sciences of anatomy, biomechanics, physiology, and psychology. An example of potential energy is a runner at the starting blocks waiting for the gun to go off. Once the starting shot is fired, the runner takes off, and the potential energy is converted to kinetic energy.

Because of electrical impulses (energy) sent from the brain through the nervous system, you are able move your muscles, and therefore, move your body. It is also because of the electrical impulses sent from the brain that movement occurs, which turns potential energy into kinetic energy.

The Western viewpoint is factual and scientifically based. In other words, if results are not tangible, seen, or scientifically proven, the Western viewpoint does not acknowledge it as "real." Energy within and used by the body is derived solely from food, a tangible material that by the process of metabolism is changed into potential energy. The concept of the subtle or energy body, recognized by ancient Eastern cultures, was unheard of in the West until President Nixon returned from China in 1972 when pictures showing the practice of acupuncture surfaced.

That was forty years ago, but it has only been within the last 10 to 15 years that acupuncture has become an accepted modality for healing in the West. The Eastern cultures of India and China not only recognized the energy body within us but have also figured out how to use and harness that energy for health and healing. The energy systems identified by the Indian and Chinese cultures are discussed in the following chapters.

Chapter 2

Understanding Energy from an Indian Ayurveda Perspective

What is Ayurveda?

Ayurveda is an ancient (approximately 5,000 years old) medical science. Although much older than Western medicine, Ayurveda is considered today to be an alternative medicine. Despite how it is viewed, it is amazingly complete and holistic. Just as Western doctors of today can pick an area of expertise or specialty, such as orthopedics or pediatrics, ancient Ayurveda doctors could choose one of the eight specialties within the Ayurveda discipline:

- **Internal medicine**–Related to the soul, mind, and body. This is similar to Psychosomatic Theory of today.
- **Ears, nose, and throat**–Identified eye diseases and surgical procedures for eye disorders such as cataracts.
- **Toxicology**–Included environmental pollution, toxins in animals and food, as well as epidemiology.
- **Pediatrics**–Included pre- and postnatal care, obstetrics, and childhood diseases.
- **Surgery**–Included surgical procedures.
- **Psychiatry**–Identified and treated diseases of the mind.

- **Aphrodisiacs**–Composed of two areas of expertise. One branch focuses on infertility treatment while the other branch focuses on spiritual development (turning sexual energy into spiritual energy).
- **Rejuvenation**–Included ways to prevent disease and gain longevity of life.

Ayurveda Energies

Within Ayurveda, there are three distinct energy systems. They are the *gunas*, the *doshas*, and the *vayus*. The gunas are the three principles that uphold all life: creation, maintenance, and dissolution. The doshas and vayus live under the umbrella of the gunas. The doshas are a person's constitution. The vayus are the energy channels in which the *prana*, the Indian word for your energy and life force, is distributed.

Gunas

The three gunas are *sattva, rajas,* and *tamas*. These three energies serve as an umbrella for all other energies and permeate throughout nature. That is, they are separate and identifiable, yet other energies always have the gunas' characteristics too.

The *Bhagavad-Gita,* also known as the *Gita*, is an ancient scriptural Indian text. The Gita defines sattva as pure, and illuminating. Sattva is balance and maintenance. The *Gita* defines rajas as full of passion and intense desire. Activity and movement is used to describe rajas energy. The Gita defines tamas as dissolution and darkness. It is the slowing down or death of something.

These three energies are constantly occurring even within your own body. One example would be cellular activity. Cells are created (rajas), live (sattva), and die (tamas) every second within your body. All are equal and needed for life to occur. However, each guna tries to be supreme by suppressing the other two.

Doshas

Five Element and Tri-Dosha Concept

Ever wonder why when you're planting flowers and digging in the dirt or having the wind and water gently spray you on a sailboat ride you feel a sense of connection and joy? It's because we are made of these very elements. Ayurveda observed this and its foundation is based on the *five elements*, which are earth, water, fire, air, and space. Each element has its unique characteristics listed in Table 2.1, and is subject to the energies of rajas, sattva, and tamas.

Element	Characteristics
Earth	Heavy, dense, slow changing, solid
Water	Liquid, cold, soft
Fire	Heat, dryness, penetration
Air	Dryness, movement
Space	Transparency, lightness, hollowness

Table 2.1

The three doshas called *vata, pitta,* and *kapha* are energies that define a person's physical and mental constitution. The doshas are made up of a combination of the five elements. The vata dosha is made up of a combination of the elements air and space. The pitta dosha is made up of a combination of the elements water, fire, and air. The kapha dosha is made up of a combination of the elements earth and water. Each person has all three doshas; however, everyone is predominately made up of one or more doshas. The combinations are: vata, pitta, kapha, vata-pitta, pitta-kapha, kapha-vata, vata-pitta-kapha (tridoshic).

Vata

Vata is the energy of motion or movement. Vata energy lives in the head and is contained within the spaces and channels of the body. Being comprised of air and space, vata is associated with wind. Like wind, vata moves and governs movement. Physical movements, psychological movement, flow, circulation, and activities of the nervous system are under vata's control. Vata governs prana, the life force within us, and rules over pitta and kapha. Vata is further broken down into *subdoshas*. The subdoshas of vata are known as the vayus discussed later in this chapter.

Pitta

Pitta is the energy of change and transformation. Pitta energy lives in the torso and is contained within the protective water of the body such as the digestive juices. Being comprised of fire and water, pitta is associated with heat. Pitta governs your metabolism digestion, hormones, and biochemical reactions. Pitta is broken down into subdoshas, called the *biles of pitta*. The subdoshas of pitta are *pachaka, ranjaka, sadhaka, alochaka,* and *bhrajaka*. Although pitta's subdoshas are not energy like the subdoshas of vata they do have specific roles and responsibilities.

Pachaka extracts the nutrients or the essence from food. Ranjaka plays a vital role in the formation of blood and gives color to lymph. Sadhaka is responsible for memory, intellect, enthusiasm, and self-esteem. The role of the alochaka pitta is recognition of color and form. Lastly, bhrajaka is responsible for maintaining the body's temperature.

Kapha

Kapha is the energy of construction. Kapha energy lives in the abdomen and pelvic area and is contained within the body's mass. Being comprised of earth and water, kapha provides support and structure. Kapha governs the structure of everything from the muscles and bones down to the individual cell. Kapha is broken down into *subdoshas*, called the *mucus of kapha*. The subdoshas of kapha are *avalambaka, kledaka, bodhaka, trapaka,* and *shelshaka*. Although the subdoshas of kapha are not energy like the subdoshas of vata they do, however, have specific roles and responsibilities.

Avalambaka protects and strengthens the heart. Kledaka protects the stomach and moistens the food in the stomach so that it can be broken up.

The well-being of sensory organs is the responsibility of trapaka while bodhaka moistens substances that come in contact with the tongue. The role of shelshaka is to keep the joints firm and lubricated.

Vayus

The vayus are a third and separate energy system in Ayurveda. Vayu is translated as wind and are the subdosha of vata energy further refining the function that vata performs within the body. Vata moves prana throughout the body. Therefore, the vayus identify all physical and mental movement of the body. Actions such as yawning, blinking, and belching are controlled by a specific vayu. There are forty-nine vayus altogether. However, out of the forty-nine, ten are directly responsible for mental and physical activities, and of those ten, five are principle vayus. The others are involuntary movements, such as moving food through the digestive tract.

These five vayus are also referred to as the *Five Prana Vayus*, the *Five Winds*, or *Five Vital Forces*. Each of the vayus lives and governs a specific part of the body, as illustrated in Figure 2.1.

The prana vayu is located in the head and controls the chest, throat, mind, heart, sense organs, intelligence, and psychological activities. The

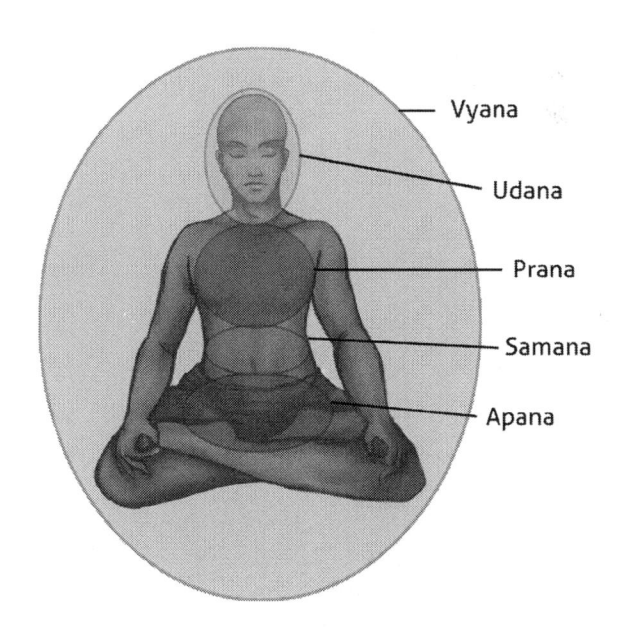

Figure 2.1

prana vayu is the captain of all the other vayus and moves along the *sushumna* channel (see Figure 3.1). It is responsible for activities such as sneezing, belching, inhalation, and swallowing. Directional movement of the prana vayu is outward.

The udana vayu is located in the throat and controls the nose, throat, and navel. Udana vayu prevents disease, regenerates, and rejuvenates the nerves as well as replenishes the body during sleep. It is responsible for the activities such as self-expression, speech, exhalation, motivation, and will power. Directional movement of the udana vayu is upward.

The samana vayu is located at the naval area and controls the alimentary tract and other abdominal organs. It is responsible for activities such as digestion and creating waste matter. Directional movement of the samana vayu is from the extremities to the core.

The apana vayu is located in the colon and controls the waist, bladder, genitals, and thighs. It is responsible for the expulsion of a fetus as well as activities such as elimination of semen, menstrual fluid, and waste matter. Directional movement of the apana vayu is downward.

The vyana vayu is located in the heart and controls the cardio-vascular system and somatic nervous system. It is responsible for activities that include movement such as walking, lifting and lowering body parts, and opening and closing the eyes. Directional movement of the vyana is throughout the body and is rapid.

Chapter 3

Understanding Energy From a Yoga Perspective

What is Yoga?

Yoga is like a diamond with many defining facets. Yoga is the science of self-knowledge. Yoga is the sister science to Ayurveda. Yoga is a philosophy. Yoga is a tool to join the mind, body, and spirit. In fact, yoga is derived from the Sanskrit word *yuj*, which means to join together. So, how does yoga join the mind, body, and spirit together? The answer is with the breath. Prana is moved via the breath and, therefore, linked closely with the breath we take in with the inhalation and expel with the exhalation. In yoga, working with the breath via specific breathing exercises and techniques is called *pranayama*.

In *Refining the Breath*, Doug Keller makes the following observations:

> *…The practice of yoga, by working the body and the breath as well as the mind, empowers us on every level by increasing the prana in the forms of the vayus.*
>
> *…Vyana vayu is strengthened by the practice of yoga asanas, through the interplay of strength and flexibility that builds a healthy sense of self…*
>
> *…The practice of yoga – both asana and pranayama are meant to optimize the functioning of these vayus as well as bring them under control, so that their energies can be used to uplift oneself.*[1]

Keller observes that yoga is an important vehicle for manipulating and maximizing the vata and vayus energies with the result being strengthened prana that creates a vibrant life force. Yoga advantageously utilizes the dosha energies of vata and the vayus. However, yoga also has its own energy system called the *chakras*.

Chakras

The word chakra means wheel or turning and comes from Sanskrit, the sacred ancient Indian language. Chakras are spinning vortices of energies. The energy of the chakras travels along channels called *nadis*. There are a total of 72,000 nadis. The three primary channels are the *sushumna, ida,* and *pingala* and are of interest here. The chakras and nadis comprise the subtle body of yoga. The subtle body is much like the wind. You can feel the wind and know it exists – it cannot be seen, just felt. It is for this reason that the Western view is skeptical if not outright rejects the validity of the Eastern energy systems, such as the chakra system.

Although the sushumna is not associated with a physical or anatomical structure, its placement corresponds with the spine. It runs vertically through the body between the top of the head and the sacrum. There are seven

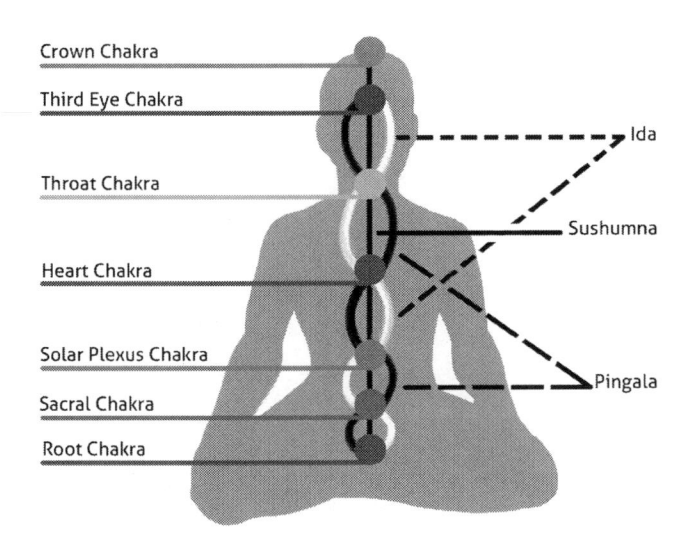

Figure 3.1

chakras that reside along the sushumna beginning at the base stacking one on top of another to the top of the head. The seven chakras are: root (first), sacral (second), solar plexus (third), heart (fourth), throat (fifth), third-eye (sixth), and crown (seventh). See Figure 3.1.

Both the ida and pingala start at the root chakra. They polarize each of the chakras, contributing to their spin. The ida begins on the left side of the root chakra, winds its way around the sushumna, and ends in the left nostril. The ida channel carries cool, calming "lunar" energy. The pingala starts on the right side of the root chakra, winds its way around the sushumna, and ends at the in the right nostril. The pingala channel carries "solar" energy and heat. The ida and pingala are analogous to the parasympathetic and sympathetic nervous systems respectively.

The chakras are aligned vertically along the sushumna. The root chakra vibrates at the lowest frequency and rotates the slowest whereas the crown chakra vibrates at the highest and rotates the fastest. The increase of vibration and rotation is greater than the previous chakra. Each chakra has its own attributes and properties such as vibration.

Root Chakra

The root chakra is the first chakra, and it is located at the base of the spine. Its color is red and its symbol is shown in Figure 3.2.

Figure 3.2

The traits associated with the first chakra are stability, survival, and security. It is associated with the earth element. The root chakra controls the kidneys and adrenal glands. The sense of smell is associated with the root chakra.

Sacral Chakra

The sacral chakra is the second chakra, and it is located in the lower abdomen. Its color is orange and its symbol is shown in Figure 3.3.

Figure 3.3

The traits associated with the second chakra are sexuality, sensuality, and creativity. It is associated with the water element. The sacral chakra governs the reproductive organs. The sense of taste is associated with the sacral chakra.

Solar Plexus Chakra

The solar plexus chakra is the third chakra, and it is located at the solar plexus, approximately two inches below the navel. Its color is yellow and its symbol is shown in Figure 3.4.

Figure 3.4

The traits associated with the third chakra are willpower, self-confidence, feelings, and power. It is associated with the fire element. The solar plexus chakra governs the pancreas organ. The sense of sight is associated with the solar plexus chakra.

Heart Chakra

The heart chakra is the fourth chakra, and it is located at the heart. Its color is green and its symbol is shown in Figure 3.5.

Figure 3.5

The traits associated with the fourth chakra are love, compassion, tolerance, and warm-heartedness. It is associated with the air element. The gland ruled by this chakra is the thymus gland. The sense of touch is associated with the heart chakra.

Throat Chakra

The throat chakra is the fifth chakra, and it is located in the throat. Its color is blue and its symbol is shown in Figure 3.6.

Figure 3.6

The traits associated with the fifth chakra are communication and truthfulness. It is associated with the ether element. The glands ruled by this chakra are the thyroid and parathyroid glands. The sense of hearing is associated with the throat chakra.

Third-Eye Chakra

The third-eye chakra is the sixth chakra, and it is located between the brows. Its color is indigo and its symbol is shown in Figure 3.7.

Figure 3.7

The traits associated with the sixth chakra are intuition, wisdom, imagination, and self-knowledge. It is associated with light. The third-eye chakra governs the pituitary gland. The sixth sense is associated with third-eye chakra.

Crown Chakra

The crown chakra is the seventh chakra, and it is located at the top of the head. Its color is purple, and its symbol is shown in Figure 3.8.

Figure 3.8

The traits associated with the seventh chakra are spirituality, enlightenment, and self-realization. It is associated with thought. The pineal gland is governed by the crown chakra. The sense of cosmic awareness is associated with the crown chakra.

Other Chakras

The seven primary charkas are located along the sushumna. However, these are not the only chakras in the body. There is one chakra located in the center of the palm and sole of each hand and foot. Whereas the primary seven chakras are classified as the major chakras, these are known as the minor chakras. Think of when you get hurt. You instinctively place a hand over the injured area. That is because the hands are one way of sending and receiving energy. The palm chakras are related and regulated by the heart chakra, which is associated with the sense of touch.

The other minor chakras are located in the sole of the feet. We take in energy from the earth through the feet. The element associated with the root chakra is earth. Therefore, these chakras are related and regulated by the root chakra.

Mudras

Mudras are a way to transmit, build, and circulate energy through the body. There are various types of mudras. There are hand, head, postural (created with yoga poses), and *bandha* (locks) mudras. The hands are the most commonly known of all the mudra types.

The hands are one of the most important parts of the body. Not only do the hands allow us to feel objects with the sense of touch, they are one of the major ways to send and receive energy. Although all cultures use hand positions, the ancient yogis realized the power held in the hands. The yogis realized the hands could be used to intensify and direct the energy of the mind within the body. Joseph Lapage classified the mudras into the following families:

- Hand gestures
- Mudras with interlaced fingers
- Body breath mudras (and mudras that touch the body)
- Mudras using the index finger and the thumb
- Fingertips in contact with the thumb
- Healing mudras for:
    - Women's issues
    - Breathing
    - Specific body areas such (e.g. back pain, joint pain)
    - Immune system
    - Purification/detoxing

- Prayer mudras
- Mudras for receiving and offering
- Mudras for meditation
- Mudras for receptive meditation

Mantras

Mantras use the energy of sound to produce an effect. A mantra is a syllable, word, or group of words. Mantra yoga is the yoga of sacred sound, which usually consists of chanting. In today's world, the meaning of mantra has evolved to mean repeating a word or phrase. Examples of mantras are affirmations and the sound *OM*. Words are energy based and powerful. When the sound of the mantra is made, physical vibrations are produced.

Regardless of ancient chanting or today's repetition, the outcome is to produce transformation via our voice. The outcome occurs on two levels. By saying the mantra, physical vibrations are produced. Over time, the effect of the vibration is that the mantra may come to have meaning associated with the effect of saying that vibration. Therefore, the first level is the energy created on the basis of the words spoken. The second level is intent. When mental intent is coupled with the vibration created, the vibration contains an additional mental component that influences the result of saying it.

Chapter 4

Understanding Energy From a Qi Perspective

What is Qi?

Qi (pronounced *chee*) means vital energy. Qi is everywhere. There are three types of Qi, of which Human Qi is discussed in this book.

- **Heaven Qi**–Considered the most important of the three. Heaven Qi governs the celestial bodies. Weather, climate, and natural disasters are controlled by Heaven Qi.
- **Earth Qi**–The vital energy of nature. Feng-Shui experts have studied Earth Qi and accumulated geomantic knowledge that gives them the expertise to help build and make decisions in regard to the Earth (e.g. where to build a house and which direction it should face).
- **Human Qi**–Your life force, and without it, you parish. When you are ill, your Qi is weak. When you are healthy, your Qi is strong.

Striving for Balance

Every energy strives to stay in balance, and so it is with Heaven, Earth, and Human Qi. When Heaven Qi becomes unbalanced, it rebalances itself through climatological events such as wind, rain, tornadoes, and hurricanes. Earth Qi is controlled by Heaven Qi. Too much rain is not good, but neither is too little rain. When Earth Qi is balanced, plants grow and animals thrive. When Earth Qi is unbalanced, earthquakes and other natural disasters occur. Human Qi is influenced by Heaven Qi and Earth Qi. When Human Qi is balanced, health is present. When Human Qi is unbalanced, illness and disease can occur.

Yin and Yang

As discussed in the previous section, Heaven Qi, Earth Qi, and Human Qi need to be harmonious and balanced. When any Qi is out of balance, instability occurs causing undesired results (e.g. hurricanes, droughts, and illness). To have balance, there must be two sides. Cold cannot be understood unless heat exists. The same is true with light and dark, as well as happiness and sadness. These two sides in Chinese philosophy are yin and yang. Neither side is better than the other. There are several symbols that represent *yin* and *yang*, however, it is most often represented by the *Taiji* illustrated in Figure 4.1.

Figure 4.1

Some important things to note about yin and yang and the Taiji symbol are as follows. Yin is represented as dark and yang is represented as light. Notice that yin contains yang (the small white circle) and yang contains yin (the small black circle). This represents that nothing is purely yin or yang. There are equal amounts of yin and yang, yet at various parts there is more of one that the other. This symbolizes that at times yin is dominant and at other times yang is dominant. The line separating yin and yang is not straight; it's curved. The curved line is a pictorial representation depicting yin is always flowing into yang, and yang is always flowing into yin.

Qualities of yin include dark, cool, slow, soft, and femininity. Qualities of yang include light, warm, fast, hard, and masculinity. In terms of energy, yin is negative, inactive, relaxing, and calming. Yang is positive, active, stimulating, and energizing.

Human Qi

Innate Qi and *Acquired Qi* are the two primary types of Human Qi. Innate Qi is what you inherited from your parents. Innate Qi is located in the kidneys. Acquired Qi is Qi that is brought into the body. There are two types of acquired Qi. *Grain Qi* which comes from the food you eat and drink. *Air Qi*, on the other hand, comes from the air you breathe. Innate Qi determines two things: the *original* duration of your life and the state of your health. Acquired Qi influences Innate Qi to determine the *actual* duration of your life and state of your health. For example, your Innate Qi may be abundant and your original life span is to live until a ripe old age. However, if you breathe polluted air, drink alcohol excessively, and eat a lot of junk food, the quality of the Acquired Qi is not good. In fact, it is bad. The effect on the Innate Qi is to shorten your life span.

There are other types of Qi that exist within the body besides the two primary ones, Innate Qi and Acquired Qi. For example, there is organ Qi. Each organ is associated with its own particular type of Qi. Liver Qi is associated with the liver; pancreas Qi is associated with the pancreas, and so on.

Meridian System

Qi flows through channels called *meridians*. The meridians are in a closed loop that has no starting or ending point. There are 14 major meridians. Twelve of the meridians are coupled, making six pairs. The pairs consist of one yin organ and one yang organ. The pairings are found in Table 4.1.

Yin Organ	Yang Organ
Lung	Large Intestine
Spleen	Stomach
Heart	Small Intestine
Kidney	Bladder
Pericardium	Triple Warmer
Liver	Gallbladder

Table 4.1

The other two meridians are the *Conception Vessel* and the *Governor Vessel*. The Conception Vessel is the main yin channel in and out of which all other yin meridians flow. The Governor Vessel is the main yang channel in and out of which all other yang meridians flow. Therefore, since these two oversee all yin and yang flow, they are not associated with a particular organ.

Chapter 5

What is Health?

The Wisdom Within

What is health? Have you ever really thought about health and what health actually is? If you are like most people, the answer is no; that you probably have not. You might define being healthy as the dictionary does:

> *The condition of being sound in body, mind, or spirit; especially: freedom from physical disease or pain*

I have thought a lot about what health is since that call from my boss so many years ago. I agree with the dictionary definition to a certain extent. I believe it is more than just the *condition*. Health has a component of intelligence. Your body has its own intelligence. It has its own wisdom. This innate intelligence and wisdom keeps you healthy, heals you when you become injured, and/or provides you with what's needed in an emergency, such as the mother lifting a car to save her child. *And it is always right*. For example, the body repairs only the damaged tissue at the injured site.

In today's modern world, many, many things have numbed the body's intelligence. In particular, modern medicine has greatly numbed the body's intelligence. Don't misunderstand me, medicine is not bad and should be taken as necessary. However, in today's world we, as a society, are pill happy. We are especially pill happy in the West. There is a pill for *everything*. Daily radio and TV commercials bombard us with a drug for this ailment or medicine for that condition. Over medicating the body numbs the body's intelligence and in the long run is usually more detrimental than letting the body heal itself. Over medicating or using medication frequently results in having the body become dependent on the medicine because the body's intelligence has been short-circuited and shuts down.

The First Step to Accessing Your Inner Power

As Dr. Deepak Chopra says in his book, *Journey into Healing*, "A shift in awareness is the first change." You must first acknowledge and accept that you can control and utilize the body's intelligence to its fullest. Once this happens, you can begin to access the power that resides within using various techniques.

There is good news. The good news is you can awaken the numbed wisdom! You can get the body's intelligence functioning at full strength! You can access your inner power! Not only can you access your inner power, but you can have more energy, be more vibrant, remove the mental fog, and actively participate in the healing process. The rest of this book describes how to do this.

Part II

Understanding Healing Traditions

Chapter 6

What is the Body?

Your Health

You are your own HMO (Health Maintenance Organization). You and you alone are responsible for your health. You and you alone live within your body 24 hours a day 7days a week. You live in your body every minute you are alive. You know your body better than anyone else, including doctors.

As Qinghsan Liu says, in *Chinese Fitness – A Mind/Body Approach*:

> *You need to care for your own health. You cannot burden your body and mind at will in order to "enjoy" life. It is also not the fault of the doctors when a very advanced illness can no longer be cured. You are responsible for your own health. It is not the task of the doctor to say: "Live it up and don't be concerned about your health. If you get sick we'll be there."* [2]

You know your body's rhythms, tendencies, and cycles. You know how your body reacts to certain things such as foods and seasons (e.g. allergy season). If you don't, the first step to staying healthy is awareness of these rhythms and cycles.

The Body Clock

Of the paradigms discussed in Chapters 1 through Chapter 4, all have developed a body clock except Yoga. Western, Ayurveda, and Chinese body clocks describe bodily functions. The Ayurveda and Chinese go into greater depth than the Western body clock that charts bodily functions.

The following three tables summarize the body clocks for these viewpoints.

Time	Bodily Function or Effect
2:00 a.m.	Deepest sleep
4:30 a.m.	Lowest body temperature
6:45 a.m.	Sharpest rise in blood pressure
7:30 a.m.	Melatonin secretion stops
8:30 a.m.	Bowel movement likely
9:00 a.m.	Highest testosterone secretion
10:00 a.m.	Highest alertness
2:30 p.m.	Best coordination
3:30 p.m.	Fastest reaction time
5:00 p.m.	Greatest cardiovascular efficiency and muscle strength
6:30 p.m.	Highest blood pressure
7:00 p.m.	Highest body temperature
11:00 p.m.	Melatonin secretion starts
11:30 p.m.	Bowel movements suppressed

Table 6.1. Western Body Clock

Time	Bodily Function or Effect	Prominent Dosha
2:00 a.m. – 6:00 a.m.	Creativity rules; dreams are most likely	Vata
6:00 a.m. – 10:00 a.m.	Body is slow after sleeping all night	Kapha
10:00 a.m. – 2:00 p.m.	Body is most active; appetite peaks	Pitta
2:00 p.m. – 6:00 p.m.	Creativity rules; most alert	Vata
6:00 p.m. – 10:00 p.m.	Body begins to slow down	Kapha
10:00 p.m. – 2:00 a.m.	Body heat is used for digestion and rebuilding tissue	Pitta

Table 6.2 Ayurveda Body Clock

Time	Dominant Bodily Occurences and Functions	Dominant Meridian
11:00 p.m.–1:00 a.m.	Sleeping and regenerating	Gallbladder
1:00–3:00 a.m.	Deep resting and dreaming	Liver
3:00–5:00 a.m.	Early stirring and gentle breathing	Lung
5:00–7:00 a.m.	Rising and defecating	Large Intestine
7:00–9:00 a.m.	Hearty eating	Stomach
9:00–11:00 a.m.	Working and thinking	Spleen
11:00 a.m.–1:00 p.m.	Eating, talking	Heart
1:00–3:00 p.m	Organizing and sorting	Small Intestine
3:00–5:00 p.m.	Storing and reserving	Bladder
5:00–7:00 p.m.	Driving and consolidating	Kidney
7:00–9:00 p.m.	Socializing, flirting, sex	Pericardium
9:00–11:00 p.m.	Relaxing and chilling	Triple Burner/ Triple Heater

Table 6.3 Chinese Body Clock

What is the Body?

To be able to take care of your body, you must understand what it is. At first when asked what the body is, you most likely answer that it is the physical anatomical structure that consists of muscles, bones, tissues, etc. This would be the Western viewpoint of the body.

Annamayakosha
BODY

Pranamayakosha
ENERGY

Manomayakosha
MIND

Vijnanamayakosha
WITNESS

Anandamayakosha
BLISS

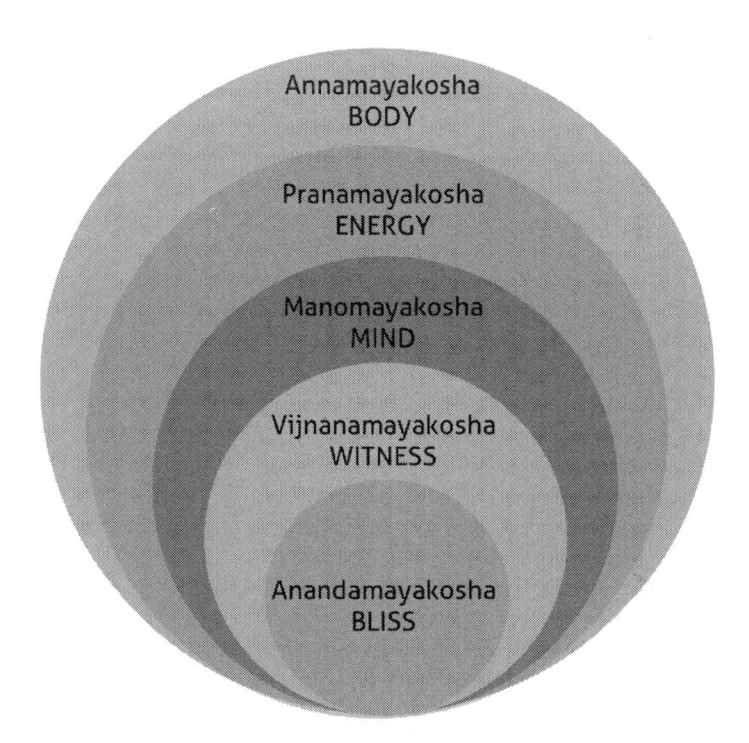

Figure 6.1

The Ayurvedic viewpoint of the body is a layered one. The layers are called the *koshas* and there are five of them. Ayurveda views the body as a multi-dimensional entity as shown in Figure 6.1.

The Ayurveda body model is similar to a Russian Matryoska doll where each resides within the previous one. The koshas, from outermost to innermost, are described in Table 6.4.

Kosha	Corresponds to
Anamayakosha	Physical body
Pranamayakosha	Energy body (flow of prana, chakras)
Manomayakosha	Emotional/Mind body
Vijnyanamayakosha	Wisdom body
Anandamayakosha	Bliss/Spiritual body

Table 6.4

Each layer or aspect of the self comprises the whole making of the body.

From the Chinese viewpoint, the mind is the body and the body is the mind. The mind and body are distinct yet integrated as one. You cannot talk of the body without talking of the mind. That is why the term psychosomatics is a foreign concept in the Chinese paradigm.

It is important to understand how the body is viewed by each paradigm to maximize healing properties and energies used within each.

Qigong and Traditional Chinese Medicine

What is Qigong?

The Chinese word for work is *gong*. Qigong, therefore, is a Chinese practice that works our vital energy strengthening our life force. Qigong evolved some 4,000 years ago from five disciplines:

- **Daoism** – A philosophy that emphasizes living in harmony with the source and essence of everything called Tao.
- **Buddhism** – A philosophy and religion based on the *Four Noble Truths*: identifies the presences of suffering, seeks the cause of suffering, the truth of the end of suffering, and attain the end of suffering.
- **Confucianism** – A philosophy based on the writings of Confucius.
- **Martial Arts** – Extensive systems of codified practices and traditions of combat that are practiced for a variety of reasons, including self-defense, competition, physical health and fitness, as well as mental, physical, and spiritual development.
- **Medical** – Maintain health and cure illness.

Traditional Chinese Medicine (TCM) was born from observation of Heaven and Earth. The four main branches of Traditional Chinese Medicine are: acupuncture, herbalism, massage, and Qigong. Today Qigong is performed as a means to stay healthy. Although there is no denying Qigong is a health benefiting exercise, Qigong includes the theories of yin/yang and the five elements.

Five Element Theory

Along with the yin/yang theory, the *five elements* theory is the foundation for the Chinese culture including Feng-Shui. The five elements are wood, fire, earth, metal, and water. There is an inherent check and balance system built-in to the five element theory. Each element either controls or supports another element in a cyclic fashion.

The controlling element takes energy away while the supporting element nourishes. The controlling cycle is metal cuts wood, wood takes nutrients from the earth, earth stops water, water extinguishes fire, and fire melts metal. The supporting cycle is wood feeds fire, fire makes earth, earth creates metal, metal attracts water, and water nourishes wood.

In Qigong, the five elements of the body are left, right, front, back, and center. The center of the body is called the *Dan Tien*. It is located approximately two inches below the navel. It is also called the lower Dan Tien as there are two others known as the middle Dan Tien and upper Dan Tien. The middle Dan Tien is located at the heart, in the center of the chest. The upper Dan Tien is located in the center of the head. When the Dan Tien is mentioned without saying where, it is the lower Dan Tien that is being referred to.

Qi and the Body

Qi affects the body in five physiological ways. Qi is the driving force that keeps the body growing and developing. Secondly, Qi keeps the fluids contained, flowing, and distributed throughout the body. Thirdly, Qi is responsible for a stable body temperature. Fourthly, Qi metabolizes food from its original form into substances used by the body. Lastly, Qi provides stability and order. For example, it is Qi that keeps the blood in the veins and urine in the bladder.

Chapter 7

Health, Vitality, and Healing the Western Way

The Western Viewpoint

Western medicine views disease and illness as either physical or mental. For the most part, Western medicine does not acknowledge that your emotional state has anything to do with creating illness that may lead to a disease. Also, Western medicine's viewpoint is that all illnesses and diseases are caused by either an external entity (i.e. virus, bacteria, or injury) or the aging process (i.e. breaking down of systems because of old age).

The Western viewpoint dictates that if a diagnosis cannot be made, then nothing is wrong and the issues you're experiencing do not exist. You have to wait until the symptoms or pain is severe enough for the Western doctor to make a diagnosis and begin treatment, such as my swollen ankle talked about in the Introduction.

The good news is once a Western doctor has a diagnosis then appropriate treatment begins. Most likely, the Western doctor prescribes some sort of medication. This can be tricky because Western doctors are specialized in their particular field. Healing of one issue may contradict the healing of another. So be sure to tell each doctor all the medicine you are taking to avoid drug interaction problems.

To stay healthy, there are some things you can do on your own such as dieting and exercising as discussed in the rest of this chapter.

Diet and Food

There are countless diets and diet books out there. Many give examples of specific foods to eat and not to eat with the end goal usually being weight loss. Many diets give you their prepackaged foods. Most count calories. Most have phenomenal results, but only for the short-term. Once off the diet, the weight creeps back up and you once again try a different diet or buy a new book promising the silver-bullet, and again you start the tumultuous losing weight/gaining weight roller coaster ride.

Here are generally accepted healthy diet guidelines, in most diet programs:
- Low fat
- No sugar
- Low carbs
- Calculate calories to be eaten (generally 300-500 calories less than what you normally eat)
- Exercise more
- Eliminate foods containing high-fructose corn syrup
- Eliminate foods containing preservatives

Many diets out there use one or more of these guidelines with their on twist to them. I'm not saying these diets are bad. What I am saying is that most of them are one-size-fits-all. These diets do not take your body into account. Each person's body is unique. The only Western diet that comes close to considering your individual make-up is *Eating Right for Your Type: The Individualized Diet Solutions to Staying Healthy, Living Longer and Achieving Your Ideal Weight* by Peter J. D'Adamo. Instead of recipes and quantities to be eaten, this book lists foods that are compatible with each blood type.

Massage

The most common form of touch therapy in the Western world is massage. Doctors write prescriptions for therapeutic massages for common injuries or ailments such as shoulder and neck pain. These types of massages are focused on the anatomical body only and do not acknowledge the energy released or the increased circulation of energy.

Reflexology is a specialized foot massage that manipulates the body's energy through massaging the feet. Although recognized by the Western world, it is not considered mainstream. Reflexology is considered alternative medicine by the West.

Increase Your Energy

In regards to health and well-being, energy is not considered vital in the Western world. Energy is only recognized as either physical or mental and is only referenced in statements of activity. Statements such as, "I wish I had as much energy as my kids," means that the kids are active for long periods of time, and "I put all my energy into the new project at work" means you put a lot of physical and/or mental energy into the new project.

Thus, to increase your energy equates to increasing the duration of a physical or mental activity. The accepted way to increase your energy might involve getting more cardiovascular exercise, sleeping more, or losing weight.

ENERGY PRACTICES

There are no energy practices in the Western world for healing. For health, you can increase your energy level by beginning an exercise routine that emphasizes and includes cardiovascular exercise. Resistance and strength training are also encouraged for overall health, not specifically as an energy increasing practice.

Accessing Your Inner Power for Healing

Sadly, the Western world ignores the healing power of the body. Instead, pharmaceutical medicine is the first choice by the overwhelming majority of Western doctors. However, the good news is that this attitude toward energy is glacially shifting. Back in 2007, Dr. Oz, a cardiothoracic surgeon and television personality, stated "energy medicine would be the next big thing."[3]

Chapter 8

Health, Vitality, and Healing the Ayurveda Way

A Question of Balance

Ayurveda is based on balance. Ayurveda states there are three causes of unbalance, which are the misuse of the mind and body, the misuse or abuse of the sensory organs, and the disregard for time and season. When the doshas are out of balance, the body becomes uneasy creating disease. Left unchecked over a period of time, the disease manifests itself. Generally, the manifestation of a disease takes a long time. The progression from unbalanced to a disease is a six-step process.

Causes of Imbalance

The first cause of an imbalance is the misuse of the mind and body. Included in the misuse of the mind and body are all thoughts and actions that disrupt the natural order of human life and cause impairment of the body, mind, emotions, and memory. Some examples are the suppression and/or excessive stimulation of natural urges, enjoyment of harmful objects and experiences, use of inappropriate force, anger, fear, greed, and intoxication.

The second cause of an imbalance is the misuse or abuse of the sensory organs. This includes the over-, under-, and/or non-stimulation of the five senses (sight, sound, touch, smell, and taste). For the eyes, this includes looking at extremely bright objects or straining the eyes by holding objects too close or too far away, or watching alarming, contemptuous, or terrifying things. Examples for the misuse of the ears include hearing loud noises, piercing cries, harsh language, or listening to insults. Abusing the sense of touch include things such as taking an excessive number of hot or cold baths, receiving a deep tissue massage as opposed to a gentle massage, and having contact or handling rough, unclean objects or objects of extreme temperatures. Noxious fumes along with strong or sharp odors are examples of misusing the sense of smell. Overindulging in a particular taste is a misuse of the sense of taste.

The third and final cause of an imbalance is the disregard for natural rhythms. There are appropriate actions for each part of the day, year, and age throughout your life. Sleeping during the day, unless prescribed, is a disregard for the natural rhythm of the day and night. An example of misuse of the season would be excessive exposure to cold during the summer.

Six Stages of Disease

As an imbalance of a dosha happens, it follows six steps to become a fully manifested disease. The steps are: accumulation, aggravation, dispersion, relocation, manifestation, and maturation. It is at the stage of manifestation that the Western doctor recognizes that something has gone awry in the body.

Accumulation

When a dosha becomes out of balance, it begins to accumulate where it lives. Vata lives in the colon, pelvic region, and bones. When vata accumulates, there can be a tendency of constipation, increased gas, dryness, and/or a sense of non-specific fear. Pitta lives in small intestine, blood, and liver. When pitta accumulates, the skin's luster disappears, there is a burning sensation throughout the body, a desire for cool things increases, and hyperacidity occurs, especially at night (e.g. acid reflux). Kapha lives in the stomach, chest, and includes secretions. When kapha accumulates, mild bloating, diminished strength, and lethargy occur.

Aggravation

At this stage, the doshas accumulation is increasing. The doshas are still in their sites and have not extended beyond into adjacent tissues. Accumulated symptoms are intensified.

Dispersion

It's at this stage the dosha is no longer contained to its original site. The doshas first enters the blood, which then carries them in any direction that is the path of least resistance. Accumulated symptoms are greatly intensified. Additional vata symptoms could include headaches, anxiety, eczema, joint stiffness, low back pain, pronounced fatigue, abdominal pain, constipation, and/or insomnia. Additional pitta symptoms may include any or all of the following: high fevers, diarrhea, rashes, and vomiting. Additional kapha symptoms may include an increase in mucus secretions, asthma, bronchitis, depression, nausea, and/or swollen joints.

Relocation

It is at this stage, that most people seek medical help. The imbalanced dosha is firmly entrenched in other tissues.

Manifestation

It is at this stage the Western doctor can make a clear diagnosis of the condition, illness, or disease. A diagnosis of diabetes, high blood pressure, and arthritis, for example, is given at this point.

Maturation

During the maturation stage is when quality of life is affected because the unique complications of the disease are fully developed.

Guna and Food

Chapter 2 defined the gunas, sattva, rajas, and tamas. Food is energy and contains the energies of the gunas. Sattvic food is pure and organic, whereas rajas food is activating and stimulating while tamas food is just the opposite. Foods have other guna characteristics, such as hot or cold. Table 8.1 lists the other guna characteristics food can have and identifies them as either rajas or tamas.

Rajas	Tamas
Hot	Cold
Hard	Soft
Dry	Oily
Light	Heavy
Sharp	Dull
Subtle	Gross
Rough	Slimy
Liquid	Solid
Transparent	Turbid

Table 8.1

Table 8.2 lists what the effect the guna has on each dosha.

Guna	Vata	Pitta	Kapha
Hot	decreases	increases	decreases
Hard	increases	decreases	increases
Dry	increases	decreases	decreases
Light	increases	increases	decreases
Sharp	increases	increases	decreases
Subtle	increases	increases	decreases
Rough	increases	decreases	decreases
Liquid	decreases	increases	increases
Transparent	increases	increases	decreases
Cold	increases	decreases	increases
Soft	decreases	increases	increases
Oily	decreases	increases	increases
Heavy	decreases	decreases	increases
Dull	decreases	decreases	increases
Gross	decreases	decreases	increases
Slimy	decreases	increases	increases
Solid	decreases	decreases	increases

Table 8.2

To be in good working order, machines need the right fuel, maintenance, and overseeing. If a car calls for premium gas and you put in regular gas, the engine will not work to its full capacity. If the oil isn't changed regularly, then it becomes gunky and the parts won't run smoothly. You need to begin to think of your body as a machine so that it runs smoothly. The next sections provide knowledge on how to use the energies to maintain health the Ayurveda way and so your body runs efficiently "on all cylinders."

Diet

If you are experiencing an accumulation of vata, then you want to eat foods that decrease vata. See Table 8.2 for food characteristics that decrease vata. A pacifying vata diet would include warm foods as well as sweet, sour, and salty foods. Avoid light, dry, and crunchy foods, such as cereal and granola.

If pitta is accumulated and pitta imbalance symptoms are evident, then you want to eat foods that decrease pitta. See Table 8.2 for food characteristics that decrease pitta. A pitta pacifying diet would include cool to lukewarm beverages and foods that are sweet, bitter, and astringent. Avoid hot and spicy foods.

If kapha is accumulated, then you want to eat foods that decrease kapha. See Table 8.2 for food characteristics that decrease kapha. A kapha calming diet would include lighter foods and foods having a pungent, bitter, and astringent taste. Light, dry, and crunchy food is recommended.

Six Tastes

According to Ayurveda, foods have six distinct tastes. These tastes relate to the five elements of earth, water, fire, air, and space. Because the doshas are comprised of these elements, each taste has an effect on each dosha. Sweet contains the elements of earth and water. Foods such as sugar, starch, cream, ghee, butter, rice, wheat, and grapes are considered sweet. The sweet taste produces a tonic and soothing effect as well as a mild laxative effect. Salty contains the elements of fire and water. Salty refers to table and sea salt. The salty taste is stimulating. Lemons and citrus fruit, cheeses, and vinegar are types types of food considered sour which contain the elements of earth and fire. The sour taste is also stimulating. Hot spices are pungent and contain the element of fire and air. They have the effect of decongesting and are diuretic. Pungent is also stimulating. Green leafy vegetables and coffee have a bitter taste. Bitter contains the space and air elements. Bitter is detoxifying, diuretic, and restores normal function. Examples of the astringent taste are found in food such as beans, persimmons, and unripe bananas. The astringent taste contains the earth and air elements and has a contracting effect. For example, it can help to coagulate blood and make bleeding stop.

Taste can be a used as vehicle to create and maintain a balance among the doshas. Therefore, each meal should include all six tastes. Taste is important for two other reasons, one being that taste fuels and energizes prana, your life force. The other being that tastes enhanced by the water element stimulate the nervous system.

Accessing Your Inner Power via The Doshas

Diseases of the Doshas

When the doshas are balanced, the body and mind are harmonious and at ease. When aggravated for a period of time, the body becomes uneasy and is at dis-ease. When at unease for a long time, illness and disease manifest. Each dosha is associated with particular ailments, illnesses, and diseases. The ailments and ways to harness your inner power to alleviate and potentially eliminate the ailment of the dosha are discussed here.

Below is a list of common ailments for each dosha. The lists are not exhaustive. Besides using the information provided in this book, it is recommended to see an Ayurvedic doctor or practitioner for the exact prescription of foods, herbal medicine, massages, and practices.

COMMON VATA AILMENTS
- Cracking of the nails
- Cracking of the feet

- Foot pain
- Sciatica
- Stiffness (e.g. ankle, back, neck)
- Rectal prolapse
- Pelvic girdle pain
- Diarrhea
- Griping abdominal pain
- Chest pain
- Eye pain
- Toothache
- Anosmia
- Tinnitus
- Headache
- Fainting
- Tremors
- Facial palsy
- Insomnia
- Dryness and hardness
- Mental instability
- Temporomandibular joint pain
- Arm atrophy
- Drooping eyelid

Common Pitta Ailments

- Burning sensations of the body
- Excessive perspiring
- Muscle fatigue
- Skin ailments (cracking, burning, itching)
- Itching of the skin
- Bleeds easily/hemorrhaging
- Conjunctivitis

- Jaundice
- Pharyngitis
- Foul odor of the mouth and/or body
- Greenish-yellowish color of the eyes, urine, or feces
- Excessive thirst
- Fainting

Common Kapha Ailments
- Excessive sleep
- Heaviness/obesity
- Indigestion
- Excessive mucus production
- Loss of strength
- Paleness
- Sweet tooth
- Salivation
- Goiter
- Anorexia Nervosa
- Excess bodily excretion
- Laziness
- Atherosclerosis
- Mucus around the heart and/or mucus in the throat

Ayurvedic Massage

An Ayurvedic massage provides many benefits. Promoting deep relaxation, an Ayurvedic massage brings balance to the mind and body. It assists in freeing toxins in the tissues and removes the toxins through the normal elimination processes of the body.

Marma Points

If the flow of prana or life force is disrupted through one or more marma point, disease will manifest. The marma points are specific areas in the body that when pressure is applied correctly, energy is tapped into and healing of the body associated with that point begins. There are 108 marma points, 107 located on the front and back of the body and one is associated with the mind. The major marma points are associated with the chakras and the other marma points are located on the torso, arms, and legs.

Ayurveda has developed a science of massage to unblock and balance the flow of prana through the marma points. These therapeutic massages apply pressure to specific marma points and are performed with various and appropriate oils to balance the dosha(s).

Oils

For an Ayurvedic massage, specific oils are used to balance the doshas. If vata needs to be balanced, use sesame oil. Other appropriate oils for vata include olive, almond, amla, bala, wheat germ, and caster. If pitta needs to be balanced, massage with coconut, sandalwood, pumpkin seed, almond, or sunflower oil. If kapha needs to be balanced, massage with either sesame or mustard oil. Safflower and corn oil may also be used for a kapha imbalance. Other oils are used for specific issues and ailments. For example, chamomile is used for muscle pain.

Energy Practices

Yoga is the sister science to Ayurveda. Asanas help balance the three doshas and five vayus. Picking the right yoga practice for balance is essential.

Vata Dosha and Yoga

When vata is rajas, choose a yoga practice that is grounding and calming. Hatha and restorative yoga would be appropriate. However, if vata is tamas, a more active style such as Qi Infused Yoga, vinyasa, or power yoga is recommended. When balanced, Qi Infused Yoga is recommended as it is a flowing practice, yet also grounding, thus making it ideal by giving vata the movement required yet the stability as well. Anusara would be another good choice. Anusara is flowing and light-hearted yet works alignment of the body, which grounds the mind during practice.

Pitta Dosha and Yoga

When pitta is over active, there is too much heat in the body and/or mind. Therefore, avoid active and heated types of yoga, and lean toward a more calming and cooling practice, such as Qi Infused Yoga, Yin Yoga, or a gentle yoga practice. On the other hand, if pitta is low, the fire needs to be built up. Bikram, hot yoga, Ashtanga, and power yoga are recommended. When balanced, pitta tends towards heated practices such as those mentioned above. Just make sure not to get too competitive and add some cooling and/or heat releasing asanas such as pigeon, camel, and fish poses into the practice to balance it out and have a well-rounded practice.

Kapha Dosha and Yoga

When kapha is in excess, lethargy and sluggishness are in abundance. Avoid gentle, Restorative, Yin Yoga and slow moving classes, and focus on classes such Qi Infused Yoga and vinyasa classes. If kapha is weak, then these are the types of classes needed. A balanced kapha would enjoy Qi Infused Yoga as well as Iyengar, Anusara, and Hatha classes.

Chapter 9

Health, Vitality, and Healing the Yoga Way

Energy Yoga Practices

Yoga is many things. In Chapter 3, yoga is defined as the science of life. Yoga also is a tool for maintaining and promoting health and healing. Health, vitality, and healing are accomplished with a regular yoga and meditation practice as well as balancing the energy of the chakras. There are many yoga styles. The following types of yoga are listed because they have a component that directly works with your body's energy.

Qi Infused Yoga

Qi Infused Yoga is a yoga that I developed and is explained in Chapter 11.

Kundalini

Kundalini is a stored energy located at the base of the spine. It is represented by a coiled snake. When kundalini is awakened via asana, pranayama, and meditation, it arises winding around the sushumna along the pathways of the ida and pingala. These ignite and fuel the chakras.

Acu-Yoga

Acu-Yoga utilizes four main types of acupressure and combines these methods with yoga asanas to help increase the circulation of the life force energy. The four types of acupressure are listed in Table 9.1.

Acupressure Type	Description
Shiatsu	Uses finger pressure on a series of points holding the pressure for 3-5 seconds
Acupressure First Aid	Uses specific points to provide temporary relief
Acucises and Dō-In	Uses forms of self-acupressure that include self-massage of the muscles and points, stretching, and breathing exercises
Jin Shin	Applies prolonged pressure on key acupuncture points to balance the meridians and bodily functions

Table 9.1

Accessing Your Inner Power via The Root Chakra
Balancing

When the root chakra is balanced, you have great stamina, you have the ability to see things to conclusion, you accomplish much, and you reach the goals you've set. However, if the root chakra is unbalanced, egotism takes charge, you lack self-control, you become self-centered and lack spirituality. You are also subject to physical urges, and develop an unhealthy relationship with basics such as food.

You may need to work on the root chakra if one or more of the following is true:
- Feel you've lost trust in life
- Don't feel comfortable in your own body
- Are worried, especially about the future

- Feel as if you've lost your emotional footing
- Are easily overwhelmed by life
- Are chronically lethargic
- Don't exercise enough
- Often have cold hands and feet
- Have colon problems
- Your digestion isn't working properly
- Have a tendency toward low back pain
- Have sciatica

The root chakra is strong when structural elements are in good condition and the large intestine and elimination are working smoothly. The root chakra is anatomically associated with the:

- Lymphatic system
- Bladder
- Structural elements (bones, teeth, nails)
- Large intestine
- Elimination system
- Lower extremities (legs – feet, ankles, etc.)
- Male prostate gland

When the root chakra is out of balance, any one or a combination of the following ailments can occur:

- Digestive disorders
- Osteoporosis
- Hemorrhoids
- Leg and foot pain
- Constipation
- Varicose veins
- Lower back pain
- Anemia and other blood disorders

- Sciatica
- Stress-induced ailments
- Skeletal problems
- Allergic reactions

Accessing

Diet

If you feel ungrounded or feel you're spinning out of control, then eat grounding food to nourish the root chakra. Examples of grounding food, would be:

- **Root vegetables**–Carrots, potatoes, parsnips, radishes, beets, onions, garlic, etc
- **Protein-rich foods**–Eggs, meats, beans, tofu, soy products, peanut butter
- **Spices**–Horseradish, hot paprika, chives, cayenne, pepper, ginger

Yoga Asana

Specific yoga poses that have a grounding quality and, therefore, beneficial for the root chakra include:
- Staff
- Apanasa
- Bound Angle
- Bridge
- Locust
- Child's Pose
- Standing Poses
    - Tree
    - Eagle
    - Warrior I, II, III

- Chair
- Goddess Pose
- Prayer Squat
- Triangle

Aromatherapy

Invoking the sense of smell can be powerful. Use the following aromas and scents to strengthen the root chakra: cloves, rosemary, cypress, and/or cedar.

Mudras

Your power is literally in your hands. By holding the mudra, you spark the power of the root chakra. If you don't feel it at first, try again without force. The more you practice the mudra in a calm, relaxed state of mind and body, the easier it becomes and the power is invoked.

Figure 8.1 - Hasta Mudra 1

Figure 8.2 - Bhairava Mudra

Sound

Sound Therapy

Sound therapy uses common vowel sounds. Note the 1 and 2 should be used with the 1 and 2 of the other chakras.

1. "o" as in "go"
2. "u" as in "use"

Affirmations

Speaking an affirmation adds the energy of sound to the powerful and positive thought. Here are two examples of affirmations for the root chakra.

- I am safe
- I feel comfortable in my body

Chants

Each chakra has a specific frequency, tone, and chant associated with it. When chanting, the 'a' is pronounced "*ah*." The chant for the root chakra is *LAM*.

Maintaining

To keep the root chakra balanced, practice one or more of the following:

- Exercise regularly
- Enjoy the sunset
- Spend as much time outdoors as possible
- Spend time in nature
- Utilize the color red with clothing, flowers, fabrics, paint, etc.
- Listen to rhythmic music that emphasizes the beat of percussion instruments such as the drums
- See an energy worker

Accessing Your Inner Power via The Sacral Chakra

Balancing

When the sacral chakra is balanced, you search for new experiences. Women with a healthy sacral chakra find fulfillment in motherhood as their creativity and take joy in bringing out the best in their children. Men with a healthy sacral chakra have balance between their masculine and feminine side and are stable. If the sacral chakra is unbalanced, there is an obsession with sex and sexual pleasures and sexual frustration can lead to aggressive behavior.

You may need to work on the sacral chakra if one or more of the following is true:

- Don't enjoy life
- Don't feel sexually fulfilled
- Have a lack of appreciation for life and don't recognize its beauty
- Are too hard on yourself
- Place too much importance on discipline and self-control
- Your creativity is blocked
- Suffer from menstrual pain
- Have bladder or kidney problems

The sacral chakra is strong when the reproductive system is problem-free. The sacral chakra is anatomically associated with the:

- Genitals
- Reproductive organs
- Bladder

When the sacral chakra is out of balance, any one or a combination of the following ailments can occur:

- Menstrual pain
- Uterine, prostate, and testicular ailments
- Inflammation of the ovaries
- Cysts
- Hip pain
- Impotence
- Skin problems
- Fungus infections in the sexual organs
- Sexual ailments
- Kidney problems, including kidney stones
- Bladder and urinary problems
- Low back pain
- Digestive disorders
- Osteoporosis
- Hemorrhoids
- Leg and foot pain
- Constipation
- Varicose veins
- Low back pain
- Anemia and other blood disorders
- Sciatica
- Stress-induced ailments
- Skeletal problems
- Allergic reactions

Accessing

Diet

Foods that nourish the sacral chakra are:

- **Sweet fruits**–Melons, mangos, strawberries, passion fruit, oranges, coconut,
- **Honey**
- **Nuts**–Almonds, walnuts
- **Spices**–Cinnamon, vanilla, carob, sweet paprika, sesame seeds, caraway seeds, pepper

Yoga Asana

Beneficial asanas for the sacral chakra include:

- Cow's Head Pose
- Bound Angle
- Seated Straddled Forward Bend
- Frog
- Apanasana
- Happy Baby Pose
- Lotus
- Locust
- Pigeon
- Prayer Squat
- Seated Hero
- Splits
- Warrior poses
- Twists
- Sphinx
- Bow

Aromatherapy

Invoking the sense of smell can be powerful. Use the following aromas and scents to strengthen the sacral chakra: sandalwood, myrrh, bitter orange, pepper, and vanilla.

Mudras

Your power is literally in your hands. By holding the mudra, you ignite the power of the sacral chakra. If you don't feel it at first, try again without force. The more you practice the mudra in a calm, relaxed state of mind and body, the easier it becomes and the power is invoked.

Figure 8.3 Hasta Mudra 2

Figure 8.4

Sound

Sound Therapy

Sound therapy uses common vowel sounds. Note the 1 and 2 should be used with the 1 and 2 of the other chakras.

1. "oo" as in "moon"
2. "o" as in "go"

Affirmations

Speaking an affirmation adds the energy of sound to the powerful and positive thought. Here are two examples of affirmations for the sacral chakra.

- I lovingly accept my body and my sexuality and sensuality
- I give my creativity freely

Chants

Each chakra has a specific frequency, tone, and chant associated with it. When chanting, the 'a' is pronounced "*ah*." The chant for the sacral chakra is *VAM*.

Maintaining

To keep the sacral chakra balanced, practice one or more of the following:

- Drink plenty of fluids
- Soak in a bath, swim, walk along the beach
- Begin a creative hobby
- Use the color orange
- Take up dancing
    - Belly
    - Salsa
    - Argentine tango
- If there are addictive tendencies toward food, then avoid chocolate, fruits, honey, ice cream, pastas, bread, and butter
- Listen to classical music

Accessing Your Inner Power via The Solar Plexus Chakra

Balancing

When the solar plexus chakra is balanced, you have extraordinary willpower, self-development/improvement, and are rarely dominated by fear. If the solar plexus chakra is unbalanced, you can't find peace, or contentment or relax; you are power-hungry, and you dismiss the concerns of others.

You may need to work on the solar plexus chakra if one or more of the following is true:

- Find it difficult recognizing goals and/or reaching them
- Give into others easily
- Have a hard time accepting criticism
- Let your emotions get the better of you
- Do things you later regret
- Suffer from nightmares, insomnia, anxiety
- Are prone to stomach cramps, heartburn, or often feel queasy
- Are overweight
- Have an eating disorder
- Have jealous or aggressive tendencies

The solar plexus chakra is strong when the digestive system is running smoothly. The solar plexus chakra is anatomically associated with the:

- Small intestine
- Kidneys
- Gallbladder
- Pancreas
- Liver

When the solar plexus chakra is out of balance, any one or a combination of the following ailments can occur:

- Stomach ailments
- Ulcers
- Liver, spleen, and/or gallbladder disease
- Jaundice
- Stomach ache
- Hypoglycemia
- Obesity
- Nervous disorders
- Diabetes
- Anorexia

Accessing

Diet

Beneficial foods for the solar plexus chakra are:

- **Granola and Grains**–Pastas, breads, cereal, rice, flax seed, sunflower seeds, etc.
- **Dairy**–Milk, cheeses, yogurt
- **Spices**–Ginger, peppermint, spearmint, chamomile, turmeric, cumin, fennel

Yoga Asana

Beneficial asanas for the solar plexus chakra include:

- Sun Salutation
- Half-Boat
- Boat
- Leg lifts
- Twists
- Plank

Aromatherapy

Invoking the sense of smell can be powerful. Use the following aromas and scents to strengthen the solar plexus chakra: lavender, chamomile, lemon, and anise.

Mudras

Your power is literally in your hands. By holding the mudra, you ignite the power of the solar plexus chakra. If you don't feel it at first, try again without force. The more you practice the mudra in a calm, relaxed state of mind and body, the easier it becomes and the power is invoked.

Figure 8.5

Sound

Sound Therapy

Sound therapy uses common vowel sounds. Note the 1 and 2 should be used with the 1 and 2 of the other chakras.
1. "a" as in "game"
2. "o" as in "ought"

Affirmations

Speaking an affirmation adds the energy of sound to the powerful and positive thought. Here are two examples of affirmations for the solar plexus chakra.

- I use my inner power to make the world a better place
- I feel calm and peaceful

Chants

Each chakra has a specific frequency, tone, and chant associated with it. When chanting, the 'a' is pronounced "*ah*." The chant for the solar plexus chakra is *RAM*.

Maintaining

To keep the solar plexus chakra balanced, practice one or more of the following:

- Stay warm
- Enjoy the sun
- Incorporate yellow into your life
- Relax near a fireplace, light candles
- Listen to romantic music (e.g. Chopin)
- Express your feelings

Accessing Your Inner Power via The Heart Chakra

Balancing

When the heart chakra is balanced, you exert influence over the environment and people positively, radiate harmony, invoke calmness, and practice tolerance and compassion. Conversely, if the heart chakra is unbalanced, you pay attention to others more than yourself and you lose yourself in love.

You may need to work on the heart chakra if one or more of the following is true:

- Have a hard time letting others into your life
- Feel lonely or isolated
- Have relationship problems
- Have difficulty sustaining friendships
- Social situations leave you worn out
- Have a hard time accepting yourself
- Have coronary, circulatory, or respiratory problems
- Are very susceptible to colds
- Have serious skin problems

The heart chakra is strong when the cardiopulmonary system is problem-free. The heart chakra is anatomically associated with the:

- Lungs
- Heart
- Arms
- Pericardium
- Hands

When the heart chakra is out of balance, any one or a combination of the following ailments can occur:

- Coronary illness
- Angina

- Arrhythmia
- Heart attack
- High/low blood pressure
- Elevated cholesterol
- Colds/allergies
- Backache in rib cage area
- Shoulder pain
- Rheumatism in the hands and arms

Accessing

Diet

Foods that nourish the heart chakra are:

- **Leafy vegetables**–Spinach, kale, dandelion greens, etc.
- **Air vegetables**–Broccoli, cauliflower, cabbage, celery, squash, etc.
- **Liquids**–Green teas
- **Spices**–Basil, sage, thyme, cilantro, parsley

Yoga Asana

Beneficial asanas for the heart chakra include:

- Revolved Triangle
- Staff
- Reverse Plank
- Sphinx
- Bow
- Camel
- Fish
- Upward Facing Bow
- Cobra
- Upward Facing Dog

Aromatherapy

Invoking the sense of smell can be powerful. Use the following aromas and scents to strengthen the heart chakra: tarragon, cloves, rose, and jasmine.

Mudras

Your power is literally in your hands. By holding the mudra, you ignite the power of the heart chakra. If you don't feel it at first, try again without force. The more you practice the mudra in a calm, relaxed state of mind and body, the easier it becomes and the power is invoked.

Figure 8.6 - Anjali Mudra

Figure 8.7 - Vajrapradama Mudra

Sound

Sound Therapy

Sound therapy uses common vowel sounds. Note the 1 and 2 should be used with the 1 and 2 of the other chakras.

1. "a" as in father
2. "a" as in father

Affirmations

Speaking an affirmation adds the energy of sound to the powerful and positive thought. Here are three examples of affirmations for the heart chakra.

- I am loving and compassionate
- I look past the surface to the deeper essence of each person
- My heart is open to giving and receiving

Chants

Each chakra has a specific frequency, tone, and chant associated with it. When chanting, the 'a' is pronounced "*ah*." The chant for the heart chakra is *YAM*.

Maintaining

To keep the heart chakra balanced, practice one or more of the following:

- Treat yourself in a loving manner
- Take care of others
- Bring green into your life
- Embrace and/or comfort others
- Allow others to touch you (e.g. get a massage)
- Listen to heart-felt music
- Listen to others
- Help others when asked

Accessing Your Inner Power via The Throat Chakra

Balancing

When the throat chakra is balanced, you are a good communicator and a master of language. You are also able to see patterns, are able to synthesize information, and have a highly developed intellect. If the throat chakra is unbalanced, you are compelled to speak the truth but through tunnel vision, you equate truth as an absolute, and you have a hard time seeing other's point of view.

You may need to work on the throat chakra if one or more of the following is true:

- Have difficulty expressing yourself
- Can't find the right words to share your thoughts and feelings
- Feel shy or inhibited when people are around
- Say things you regret later
- Have a speech defect
- Don't feel inspired by your work
- Have a hard time telling the truth and often tell "white" lies
- Suffer from abnormal thyroid conditions (e.g. hypothyroidism, hyperthyroidism)
- Often have sore throats
- Suffer from neck or shoulder pain

The throat chakra is anatomically associated with the:
- Neck
- Jaw
- Larynx
- Esophagus
- Windpipe
- Voice
- Thyroid

When the throat chakra is out of balance, any one or a combination of the following ailments can occur:

- Throat pain
- Tonsillitis
- Neck vertebrae issues
- Neck and shoulder pain including stiffness
- Over or under active thyroid

Accessing

Diet

Foods that nourish the throat chakra are:

- **Liquids in general**–Water, fruit juices, herbal teas
- **Tart or tangy fruits**–Lemons, limes, grapefruit, kiwi
- **Other tree growing fruits**–Apples, pears, plums, peaches, apricots, etc.
- **Spices**–Salt, lemon grass

Yoga Asana

Beneficial asanas for the throat chakra include:

- Bridge
- Yoga Mudra
- Half-Shoulderstand
- Half-Plough
- Shoulderstand
- Plough
- Fish

Aromatherapy

Invoking the sense of smell can be powerful. Use the following aromas and scents to strengthen the throat chakra: peppermint, camphor, and eucalyptus.

Mudras

Your power is literally in your hands. By holding the mudra, you ignite the power of the throat chakra. If you don't feel it at first, try again without force. The more you practice the mudra in a calm, relaxed state of mind and body, the easier it becomes and the power is invoked.

Figure 8.8

Figure 8.9 - Pushpaputa Mudra

Sound

Sound Therapy

Sound therapy uses common vowel sounds. Note the 1 and 2 should be used with the 1 and 2 of the other chakras.

1. "i" as in "kite"
2. "a" as in "game"

Affirmations

Speaking an affirmation adds the energy of sound to the powerful and positive thought. Here are examples of affirmations for the throat chakra.

- I use the power of words to make the world a better place
- It becomes easier each day to express what I think and feel

Chants

Each chakra has a specific frequency, tone, and chant associated with it. When chanting, the 'a' is pronounced "*ah*." The chant for the throat chakra is *HAM*.

Maintaining

To keep the throat chakra balanced, practice one or more of the following:

- Take voice training or public speaking lessons
- Keep a journal
- Expose yourself to blue colors in nature (e.g. look at the sky, ocean)
- Develop courage to hold to your own opinions in a nonaggressive and noncombative way
- Practice mantra yoga

Accessing Your Inner Power via The Third-Eye Chakra

Balancing

When the third-eye chakra is balanced, you have a thirst for knowledge, easily see falsehoods, and you experience inner peace. If the third-eye chakra is unbalanced, you distance yourself from others, which can lead to isolation, depression, and mental and emotional illness.

You may need to work on the third-eye chakra if one or more of the following is true:

- Feel life is meaningless
- Suffer from anxiety or depression
- Can't hear your inner voice
- Have a hard time concentrating
- Thoughts are scattered
- Susceptible to headaches
- Have sinus, eye, and/or vision problems
- Have to strive for higher realization

The third-eye chakra is anatomically associated with the:

- Cerebellum
- Face
- Sinuses
- Hormonal system
- Nervous system
- Sensory organs of sight, hearing, and smell

When the third-eye chakra is out of balance, any one or a combination of the following ailments can occur:

- Blindness
- Eyestrain
- Blurred vision

- Headaches and migraines
- Nightmares
- Colds
- Middle ear inflammation
- Conjunctivitis
- Brain diseases
- Sinus problems
- Mental diseases

Accessing

Diet

Foods that nourish the third-eye chakra are:

- **Dark bluish colored fruits**–Blueberries, red grapes, black berries, raspberries, etc.
- **Liquids**–Red wines, grape juice
- **Spices**–Lavender, poppy seed, bay leaf

Yoga Asana

Beneficial asanas for the third-eye chakra include:

- Downward Facing Dog
- Half-Plough
- Plough
- Bridge
- Yoga Mudra

Aromatherapy

Invoking the sense of smell can be powerful. Use the following aromas and scents to strengthen the third-eye chakra: lemongrass and violet.

Mudras

Your power is literally in your hands. By holding the mudra, you ignite the power of the third-eye chakra. If you don't feel it at first, try again without force. The more you practice the mudra in a calm, relaxed state of mind and body, the easier it becomes and the power is invoked.

Figure 8.10

Sound

Sound Therapy

Sound therapy uses common vowel sounds. Note the 1 and 2 should be used with the 1 and 2 of the other chakras.

1. "e" as in "meet"
2. "e" as in "meet"

Affirmations

Speaking an affirmation adds the energy of sound to the powerful and positive thought. Here are examples of affirmations for the third-eye chakra.

- I'm in touch with my inner power
- I listen to my inner voice

Chants

Each chakra has a specific frequency, tone, and chant associated with it. The chant for the third-eye chakra is: *OM*.

Maintaining

To keep the third-eye chakra balanced, practice one or more of the following:
- Read philosophical and spiritual material
- Keep a dream journal
- Meditate under the stars
- Wear dark blue or indigo
- Use your imagination
- Read fairy tales, fantasy, and/or mythology

Accessing Your Inner Power via The Crown Chakra

Balancing

When the crown chakra is balanced, you realize there is something greater than yourself. You inspire others and radiate positive energy. If the crown chakra is unbalanced, you withdraw from the world, are drawn to black magic, and subject to spiritual sickness or denial of a spiritual world.

You may need to work on the crown chakra if one or more of the following is true:

- You are frequently depressed
- Lack joy in life
- Suffer from chronic or life-threatening illness
- Have a weakened immune system

The crown chakra is healthy if the brain and nervous system are healthy. The crown chakra is anatomically associated with the:

- Central nervous system
- Cerebral cortex

When the crown chakra is out of balance, any one or a combination of the following ailments can occur:

- Inability to learn
- Confusion
- Apathy
- Alienation
- Depression
- Boredom
- Weak immune system
- Forgetfulness
- Sleep disorders
- Headaches

- Mental illness
- Anxiety
- Multiple Sclerosis

Accessing

Diet

Fasting and/or detoxification are recommended for the crown chakra. The incenses and smudging herbs, (i.e. herbs used for inhalation versus eating), of choice for the crown chakra include myrrh, frankincense, juniper, sage, and copal.

Yoga Asana

Beneficial asanas for the crown chakra include:
- Downward Facing Dog
- Headstand
- Handstand
- Eye exercises
- Rabbit
- Fish

Aromatherapy

Invoking the sense of smell can be powerful. Use the following aromas and scents to strengthen the crown chakra: rosewood.

Mudras

Your power is literally in your hands. By holding the mudra, you ignite the power of the crown chakra. If you don't feel it at first, try again without force. The more you practice the mudra in a calm, relaxed state of mind and body, the easier it becomes and the power is invoked.

Figure 8.11 - Kali Mudra

Figure 8.12

Sound

Sound Therapy

Sound therapy uses common vowel sounds. Note the 1 and 2 should be used with the 1 and 2 of the other chakras.

1. "ing" as in "bringing"
2. Silence

Affirmations

Speaking an affirmation adds the energy of sound to the powerful and positive thought. Here are examples of affirmations for the crown chakra.

- The essence of my being is light and peace
- I open myself to the infinite power of God

Chants

Each chakra has a specific frequency, tone, and chant associated with it. The chant for the crown chakra is *OM*.

Maintaining

To keep the crown chakra balanced, practice one or more of the following:
- Practice relaxation
- Take up mountain climbing
- Wear and use the colors of white and violet
- Meditate

Chapter 10

Health, Vitality, and Healing the Qigong Way

Movement and Stillness

Under the energies of yin and yang, if there is movement, there must also be stillness. When comparing Qigong to aerobics, Qigong it is yin. Within Qigong, the movements are yang, and meditation is yin. For the true power of Qigong to be fully realized, it needs to contain both elements of movement and stillness.

Movement and stillness are equally essential in Chinese philosophy. Water that flows smoothly through a riverbed does not become stagnant and does not accumulate silt and algae. Qi must also run smoothly through the meridian channels like water running through a riverbed. The movement of Qi occurs through movement of the body and through thought. Qigong practices that move the body generate Qi movement via the limbs and move the Qi toward the core is called the *external elixir*. On the other hand, Qi that is moved by the mind is called the *internal elixir*. With the internal elixir, Qi is cultivated at the body's core and is moved outward towards the limbs as shown in Figure 10.1.

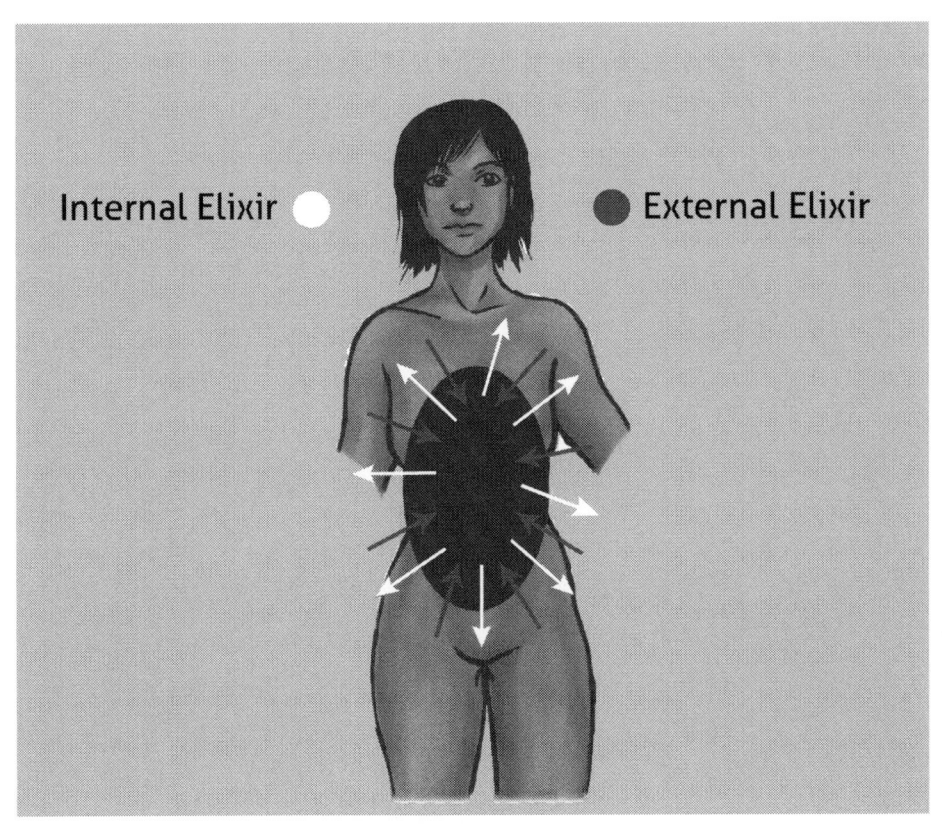

Figure 10.1

There are many types of Qigong practices that generate external elixir and internal elixir. Qi Infused Yoga is an example of an external elixir. Movement is the vehicle in Qi Infused Yoga to circulate Qi through the meridians.

Accessing Qi

Qi continually flows through the meridians. If the flow is slow, the Qi is said to be weak or stagnant. If the flow is overly strong, it is overactive. Qi can also be redistributed and flow outside its natural path. Medical Qigong is a method to remedy these issues. Medical Qigong practices include acupuncture, administration of herbal medicines, and medical massage. Diet and food are also a measure for maintaining your health. All of these medical techniques are discussed in this chapter.

Acupuncture

Acupuncture falls into the category of medical Qigong, and is considered by the West to be an alternative medicine. Acupuncture uses thin, solid needles. The needles are inserted into acupuncture points along the meridians as shown in Figure 10.2.

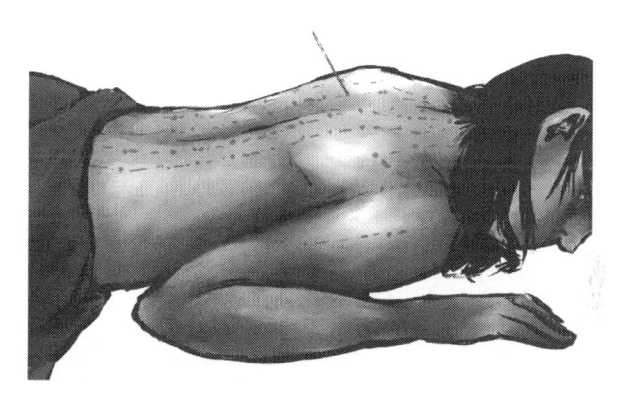

Figure 10.2

Each meridian is classified as yin or yang. Each meridian, except for the Governor's Channel and Conception Vessel, is associated with an organ of the body and it is named after that organ. For example the liver meridian is named after the liver organ.

When Qi is stagnant or slow, organs weaken and disease manifests over time. Acupuncture is a Qigong TCM technique that gets stagnant Qi flowing.

Chinese Massage

Chinese massage is not acupressure. Acupressure is a Japanese practice; however, acupressure is derived from Chinese massage. Chinese massage comes in three flavors, which are massaging the muscles, massaging the acupuncture points, and massaging the nerve and channel endings.

Muscle Massage

When you are tired and your muscles ache, you probably go to a spa and get a massage. It not only relaxes the muscles, but you feel energized as well. According to the Chinese, this is because stagnant or blocked Qi begins to flow again; blood circulation is increased, which nourishes the muscles. Various techniques such as rubbing, grasping, shaking, pressing, sliding, or slapping the muscles may be involved.

ACUPUNCTURE MASSAGE

The idea behind this type of massage is to massage the acupuncture points without using needles to stimulate the Qi flow. It is very similar to the Japanese technique of acupressure. The same principles and results apply to an acupuncture massage as to acupuncture. That is, stimulate Qi channels to help circulate the energy locally.

What's known as reflexology in the West, is the second type of acupuncture massage. This type of massage involves rubbing and pressing the endings of the nerve and Qi channels. While muscle massage feels good, releases tension, and gets stagnant Qi flowing again, rubbing and massaging the nerve endings, theoretically, stimulates and benefits the organs leading to overall better health.

Diet

The Chinese view on food is completely different from the Western view. Over processed Western food is the primary reason for the rise in obesity in China. Until very recently, obesity was virtually unheard of in China.

Chinese food that is properly prepared is good for helping you to maintain and sustain life as well as fight off disease. However, Chinese fast food smothered in MSG, oils, and heavy meats have the opposite effect. A 1990 survey discovered the Chinese consumed 30% more calories than Westerners yet did not gain as much weight. Why? The answer is their mindset. The Chinese view food as nourishment and a source of Acquired Qi, not as potential for gaining weight. Other major mindset differences include:

- **Meat vs. Vegetables**–In the West, the meat is the center of the meal or main dish and all other dishes complement and go with the meat. The reverse is true for the Chinese. The vegetables are the main dish with a little bit of meat added to them.

- **Potatoes vs. Rice**–Potatoes and noodles are the staple dishes that flank the main dish of meat in the West. However, rice is the staple for the people of China. Whereas potatoes and noodles are high in starch and simple carbohydrates, rice is just the opposite. Rice is highly nutritional and certain types of rice are high in fiber, such as brown rice.

- **Soup**–Soup or watery porridge is present at every Chinese meal. Liquid food is highly beneficial because it helps to control the appetite and keeps you hydrated. Soups are an accessory and generally served as an appetizer in the West. Therefore, a traditional Western meal tends to be dry. Consequently, Westerners are urged to drink more water to compensate for the lack of liquid in the Western diet.
- **Overcooked vs. Lightly Cooked**–Even though cooking destroys nutrients, raw vegetables are hard on the body. Lightly cooked food, such as steamed or stir-fried food, is easy to digest and most of the nutrients are intact.
- **Yin/Yang Cooking**–Everything is balanced. Neither too much yin in food nor too much yang is good for you. A well-cooked Chinese meal has equal portions of each. Yin foods are wet and moist while yang foods are dry and crisp. Examples of yin food are cucumber, banana, celery, brown rice, and milk. Examples of yang food are peppers, mangoes, leek, walnut, and grapes.

Part III

Qi Infused Yoga

Chapter II

Qi infused Yoga

The Need for Qi Infused Yoga

In 1946, the birth rate soared when the troops returned after World War II. The high birth rate continued until 1964. Those born during this period of time became known as the *baby boomers*. As of 2012, baby boomers range in age from 48-66 years old. Due to various reasons, the baby boomers of 2012 are generally healthier than those of the same age 50 years ago. Baby boomers are expected to live longer than the generation before them as well. The baby boomers are also the largest population in the United States at the moment.

While growing up, the majority of baby boomers did not know about yoga. If they did, it was shrouded by mysticism. It wasn't until the early 1990's that yoga started to gain popularity and momentum in the United States. I know when I moved to North Carolina in 1999 there were only two yoga studios in the area. Now, 13 short years later, there are yoga studios everywhere and yoga classes offered at every gym. Yoga is commonplace now. Yoga is mainstream. This is great news because yoga is a physically, mentally, and emotionally beneficial practice.

However great news this is, it causes a dilemma for the baby boomer/older adult who wants to try yoga for the first time. Generally, in good health, but having normal wear-and-tear on their bodies, baby boomers experience classes geared for the younger adult crowds consisting of 20-30 year olds. That's because the fitness industry caters to young adults and virtually ignores the baby boomer generation. Added to this, most yoga magazines and books show a younger practitioner doing some intimidating pretzel-type poses. A few books, such as Richard Rosen's *Yoga for 50+*, have been published recently but it can still be intimidating even with the modifications given.

While teaching yoga at local gyms and health clubs, I would frequently be asked by older adults, how yoga could be done safely because of a particular injury or ailment from which they suffered or how to practice yoga when they have a chronic condition such as low back pain. Rightly so, they are apprehensive because of their conditions and do not want to have a flare up or reinjure themselves.

I would also be asked how yoga could be utilized to relieve pain. They had heard yoga was a wonderful pain management tool – which it is. Those living with chronic pain are desperate to find relief, yet are extremely fearful of trying anything that has a chance of elevating their pain level. A gym yoga class does not take injured and those living with constant pain into consideration.

Hearing my client's concerns over and over coupled with being a baby boomer myself, I can definitely relate. Even though I have been practicing yoga since 1992, my body is not the same as it was 20 years ago. I also admit I have old injuries that can and do flare up. Given the continual questions and not being able to guide them to a suitable class, I developed an active yet kinder and gentler yoga style for the baby boomers. Qi Infused Yoga was born.

What is Qi Infused Yoga?

So, what is Qi Infused Yoga? Quite simply, Qi Infused Yoga is a style of yoga that blends the practices of Qigong, Tai Chi, and yoga into a fluid practice. Qi Infused Yoga is a practice that has equal focus on physical movement and the movement of energy. Qi Infused Yoga gets the energy flowing through the meridians and the chakras, is easy on the joints, and works the muscles but not to the point of no return as in aerobic or group fitness yoga classes. Qi Infused Yoga infuses the gentle flowing movements of Qigong, Tai Chi, and yoga asanas that leaves you feeling cool, calm, refreshed, and energized. Anyone can practice Qi Infused Yoga, but it was created for older adults who are generally in good health but are experiencing the normal wear and tear that aging brings.

Comparing Qigong and Yoga

Qigong and yoga are similar as they are both considered mind/body practices. They both consider breath essential. Table 11.1 summarizes some key comparisons between the two Eastern practices.

	Qigong	**Yoga**
Breathing	Good breathing is without sound and causes little or no sensations or movement of the nostrils. There are three types: natural breathing, abdominal breathing, and reverse breathing.	Yoga's breath discipline is pranayama. Breath can be audible and runs the spectrum from heating to cooling.
Focus of the movement or asana	Get stagnant Qi moving and strengthen the Qi.	Proper alignment of the asana pose.
Meditation	Reach a meditative state of a clear, focused, and calm mind before practice. As a separate practice, the goal of meditation is to guide and circulate the Qi consciously.	Generally, a yoga practice starts with asana. The asana practice is considered the way you prepare for meditation.
Movement	Movement is required and is of a flowing and rhythmic nature.	Yoga involves very little, if any, movement. Yoga is based on static poses held for varying periods of time with the notable exception of the Vinyasa style of yoga.
Origins	Dates back approximately 5,000 years, Qigong's and TCM's heritage is founded on the philosophical principles from the I Ching, The Book of Changes.	Dates back approximately 8,000 years and are from ancient Vedic texts Rigveda, Yajurveda, Samaveda, and Atharaveda. The Bhagavad Gita is also considered to be a sacred text.

Table 11.1

Asanas

Apanasana

Lie on your back. Bend the knees and bring them to the chest. Wrap the hands around the knees. Keep the chin parallel to the floor.

Bound Angle Pose

Sit tall pressing the buttocks into the mat and lifting the heart forward and up. Press the soles together and hold the ankles or feet.

Cat Pose

Begin on hands and knees with the hands in line with the shoulders and the knees in line with the hips. Begin to arch the back, like an angry cat, by tucking the chin and tailbone under. Draw the navel toward the spine.

Cat Stretches – From Cat, bring the knee to the nose and stretch leg behind you as you look up.

Chaturanga

From a prone position with the legs and arms straight, bend the elbows and lower down to an inch above the ground.

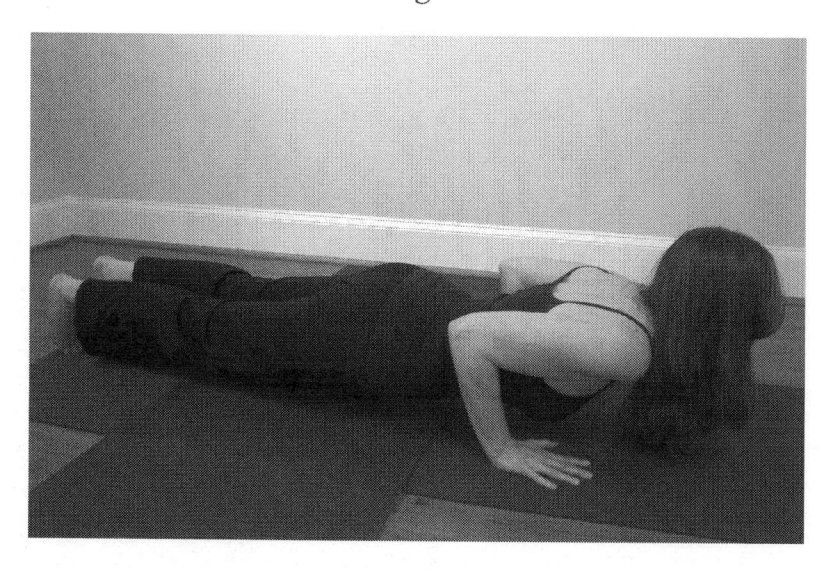

Child's Pose

From a kneeling position, lower the forehead to the mat. Place the hands beside the feet.

Cow Pose

Begin on the hands and knees with the hands in line with the shoulders and the knees in line with the hips. Tip the chin and tailbone toward ceiling while releasing the navel toward the mat.

Corpse Pose

Lie in a comfortable position, legs can either be straight or the knees can be bent. Rest the arms beside the body with the palms facing upward. Close the eyes and relax the muscles.

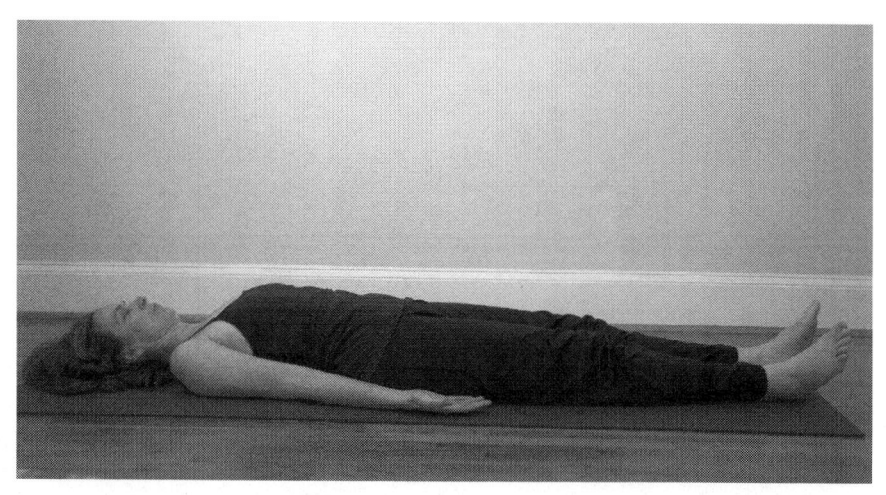

Cow's Head Pose

Legs: Sit on the floor with the knees bent toward the ceiling. Lower the left knee to floor and bring the foot underneath the right leg toward the right hip. Place the right foot on the outside of the left knee. Stack the knees while sliding the feet away from the hips. Feet should be equal distance from the hips.

Arms: Raise the right arm to ceiling and bend the elbow. Reach the left arm down and bend the elbow. Walk the left hand along the back bringing the hands together. Clasp the fingers together, if possible.

Repeat on the other side.

Downward Facing Dog

From Forward Bend, step the right foot and then the left foot behind. Roll the shoulders up, back, and down while pressing firmly into the floor with the hands. Engage the quadriceps and draw the knee caps up toward the hips. Tilt the tailbone toward the ceiling as you press the heels down.

Eagle Pose

Legs: Bend the knees slightly. Balance on *left* leg while crossing *right* leg over at the *left* thigh. Wrap the *right foot* around the *left* shin or ankle, if possible. *Arms:* Stretch the arms straight in front of you, shoulder width apart with the palms facing the ceiling. Cross the arms in front placing the *left* arm on top of the *right* arm at the elbow. Bend the elbows so that the forearms are perpendicular to the floor. Bring the back of the hands together. If possible, slide the palm of the *right* hand along the *inside* left wrist until the palms touch. Fingers point toward the ceiling.

Repeat on the other side.

Awakening Your Health and Vitality 101

Forward Bend

From Mountain pose, fold forward keeping the shoulders rolled up, back, and down and the back flat.

Goddess Pose

Separate the feet with the toes turned slightly out. Tuck the tailbone under. Bend the knees and elbows.

Half Lord of the Fish

Legs: Sit on the floor with the legs straight out in front of you. Bend the right knee and place the right foot on the outside of the left knee. Bend the left knee and draw the left foot toward the right hip.

Arms: Grow up through the spine. Begin to twist to the right. Place the left elbow on the outside of the right knee, pressing firmly into the knee. Place the right hand on the floor behind you.

Repeat on the other side.

Half Lord of the Fish – Variation

Legs: Sit on the floor with the legs straight out in front of you. Bend the right knee and place the right foot on the outside of the left knee. Left foot is flexed.

Arms: Grow up through the spine. Begin to twist to the right. Place the left elbow on the outside of the right knee, pressing firmly into the knee. Place the right hand on the floor behind you.

Repeat on the other side.

Head-to-Knee Pose

Sit on the floor with the legs straight out in front of you. Bring the right foot to the inside of the left thigh. Fold forward keeping the shoulders rolled up, back, and down and the back flat. Hold onto left leg, ankle, or foot.

Lunge Twist

Begin kneeling. Step the left foot forward and slide the right knee behind the right hip. With the shoulders over the hips, sink the hips without leaning forward. Bring the right arm to the floor and raise the left arm to the ceiling. Twist the torso to look at the left hand. Switch hands.

Repeat other side.

Mountain

Press the feet into the floor. Pull the arches and kneecaps up. Engage the quadriceps. Tuck the tailbone under. Create space between the navel and the sternum. Lift the heart forward and up. Widen through the collarbone. Roll the shoulders up, back, and down, squeezing the shoulder blades gently together. Tuck the chin in slightly. Lift up through the neck.

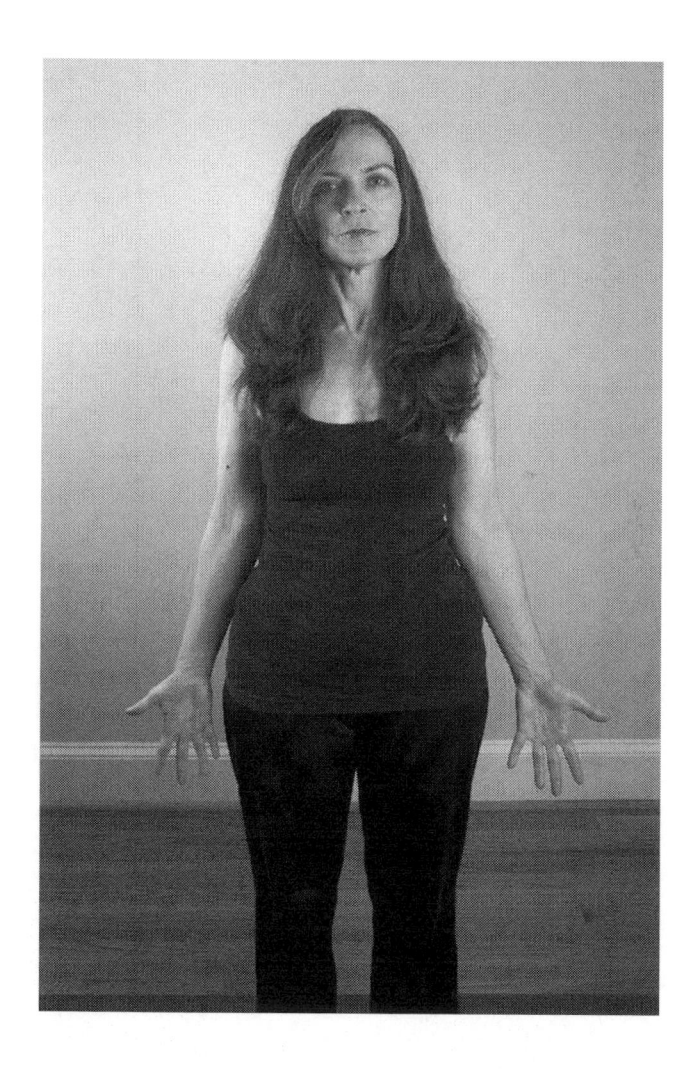

Reverse Warrior

From the Warrior II pose, drop the hand to the back leg and slide it down the leg as you lift up through the ribs and float the front arm overhead. The palm faces downward.

Repeat other side.

Side Angle Bend Pose

From the Warrior II pose, place the front forearm on the thigh of the front leg or lower the hand to the mat. Raise the other arm to the ceiling.

Repeat other side.

Straddled Forward Bend

Separate the feet wider than the shoulders. Roll the shoulders up, back, and down. Fold forward keeping the back flat. Place the hands on the legs, ankles, or mat.

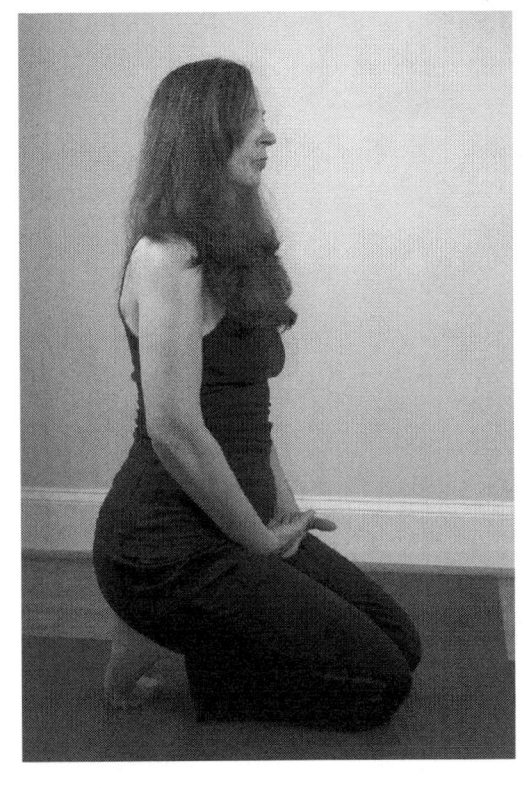

Sit on the Heels

Begin kneeling. Curl the toes under. Sit on the heels.

Triangle

Separate the feet. Turn the right foot 90 degrees. Lift the left heel and pivot away from the right foot, pointing toes inward to a 30-45 degree angle. Lift arms out to the side, shoulder height. Still facing forward, move hips to left and stretch through the ribs lowering torso parallel to the mat. Drop the right hand to the right leg or the mat and lift the left hand to the ceiling.

Upward Facing Dog

Lying in a prone position, tuck the tailbone under and engage the legs. Hands are under the shoulders. Begin to lift up from the core, with the head the last to be raised. The arms are straight or slightly bent. The hips are off the floor.

Warrior I

Separate the feet. Turn the right foot 90 degrees. Lift the left heel and pivot away from the right foot, pointing toes inward to a 30-45 degree angle. Lift the arms out to the side, shoulder height. Bend the right knee and keep the shoulders over the hips. Turn torso toward the right knee. Lift up through the ribcage and bring the arms overhead keeping the shoulders down.

Repeat other side.

Warrior II

Separate the feet. Turn the right foot 90 degrees. Lift the left heel and pivot away from the right foot, pointing toes inward to a 30-45 degree angle. Lift the arms out to the side, shoulder height. Keeping the hips facing forward, turn the head to look over the right hand as you bend the right knee.

Repeat other side.

Vinyasas and Sequences
Palm Tree Series

Step 1 and 2: Circle the arms out to the side and around; circle the arms in the opposite direction.

Step 3 and 4: Sway side-to-side with the hands together, then with the hands apart.

Step 5: Step the right foot back and lift the heel. Both knees are bent. Raise the left arm. Begin to straighten the knees and arch back lifting and stretching through the front of the body with the head being last to come back. Alternate sides.

Sun Salutation

Start with the right foot and repeat the sequence starting with the left foot.

Step 1: Start in Mountain pose. Circle the arms to the side and overhead.

Step 2: Circle the arms out to the side and fold forward into a Forward Bend.

Step 3: Step the right foot back into a Lunge.

Step 4: Step the left foot back. Bend the elbows and lower into Chaturanga.

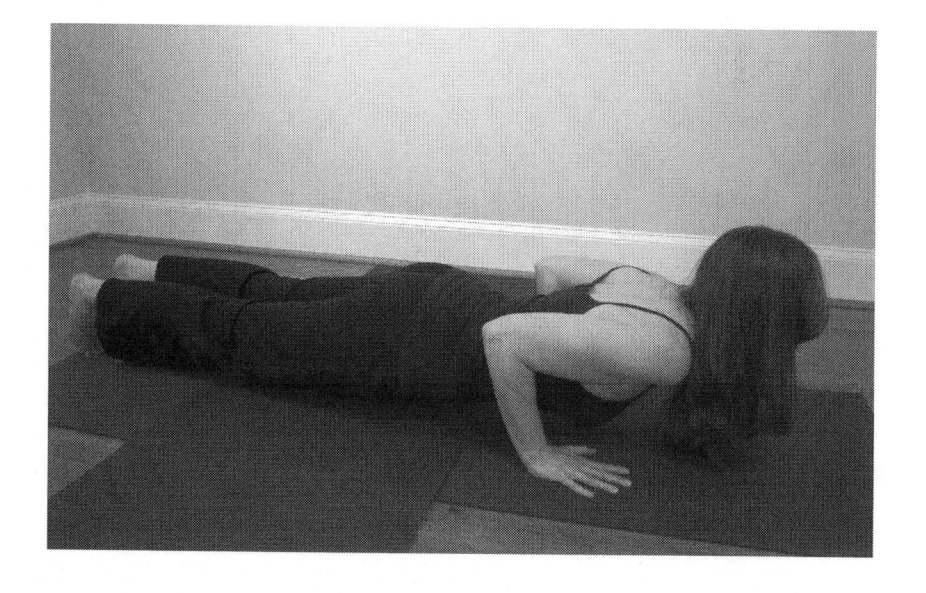

Step 5: Come forward and lift into Upward Facing Dog.

Step 6: Curl the toes under and come into Downward Facing Dog.

Finish the Sun Salutation

Step 7: Step the right foot forward into a Lunge.
Step 8: Step the left foot forward and come into a Forward Bend.
Step 9: Circle the arms to the side and come into Mountain pose.

Qigong Movements and Tai Chi Solo Forms

Qigong and Tai Chi are rhythmic and fluid. Each movement flows from one to the next without stopping between movements. In a Qigong practice, each movement is performed a maximum of six times. When crossing the wrists or hands during a Qigong practice, women cross the left on top of the right while men place the right on top of the left.

Posture

There are several postures, called stances, used in Qigong and Tai Chi. There are many stances and variations of each stance. Therefore, the stances listed are only generally described. The stances listed are also those used in the Qi Infused Practices found in Chapter 11.

- **Horse Stance** - Is named such because of the similarity to the position when riding a horse; feet are shoulder width apart.
- **Wide Horse Stance** - Start in Horse Stance and step the feet apart.
- **Bow Stance** - The front leg is bent and the back leg is stretched or straightened like a bowstring.

In addition to the stances, remember these key points:

- The tip of the tongue is placed on the roof of the mouth behind the teeth.
- When inhaling, allow the belly to expand.
- When inhaling, keep the shoulders from rising and the chest from expanding.
- Hands are cupped.
- A level of conservation is maintained with each movement. That is, during or at the end of a movement, the joints (e.g. knees, elbows) remain slightly bent.
- When practicing Qigong or Tai Chi, the mind is in a calm state.

QiGong Movements

Qigong 18 Movements

The movements flow together with no break or pause between movements and are performed sequentially.

Movement 1
Awakening the Qi

Begin in Horse Stance. Simultaneously slightly straighten the knees and float the arms up drawing the hands toward the chest. Bend the knees and float the arms down.

Movement 2
Expand the Chest

Start as you would in Awakening the Qi. When the hands are at chest level, turn the palms inward and separate the hands out to the side. Bend the knees, and bring the arms together in front of the chest and down.

Movement 3

Moving the Rainbow

Begin as you would in Expand the Chest. Continue until the arms are raised. Pivot on the left heel lifting the left toes and straighten the left leg. Shift your weight to right leg as you bend over left leg.

Repeat on the other side.

Movement 4

Pushing the Clouds Apart
Step 1

Start with arms down and wrists crossed in front of the body.

Movement 4

Pushing the Clouds Apart

STEP 2

Lift the arms up and circle out to side and back to the starting position.

NOTE: Perform Expand the Chest before moving to Rolling the Arms.

Movement 5

Rolling the Arms

As the back arm comes forward turn palm toward you while lowering the front arm down and circling behind.

NOTE: The eyes watch the hand moving back.

Movement 6

Rowing on a Calm Lake

Step 1

Reach arms back with palms facing forward.

Movement 6

Rowing on a Calm Lake

Step 2

Circle up, around, and down.

Movement 7

Lift Sun with Hands

After Rowing on a Calm Lake, bring hands to the waist with the palms facing upward. Shift your weight to left leg and sweep the right hand to the left side. Bring the right hand with palm up to shoulder height.

Repeat with the left hand.

Movement 8

Gaze Back at the Moon

Twist the torso to the left. Straighten and lift the left hand behind. Gaze at the left hand.

Repeat on the right side.

Movement 9

Turn Upper Body and Push Palms

From Horse Stance, bring the hands to the waist with the palms facing upward. Turn the torso to the left and push the right hand diagonally across the body to the left.

Repeat to the right.

Movement 10

Cloud Hands in Riding Position

Start with the palms facing inward, the right hand is at chest or at eye level, and the left hand is at the navel. Twist to the left, lowering the right hand to the navel while raising the left hand up. Twist to the right and repeat.

Movement 11

Grab From the Bottom of the Sea and Look to the Sky

Step 1

Step into Bow Stance turning the left foot out. Lean over the left knee and cross the wrists over the left knee.

Movement 11

Grab From the Bottom of the Sea and Look to the Sky

Step 2

Simultaneously, raise the torso and arch backward opening the arms out to the side. Float the arms down beside the left leg.

Repeat on the other side.

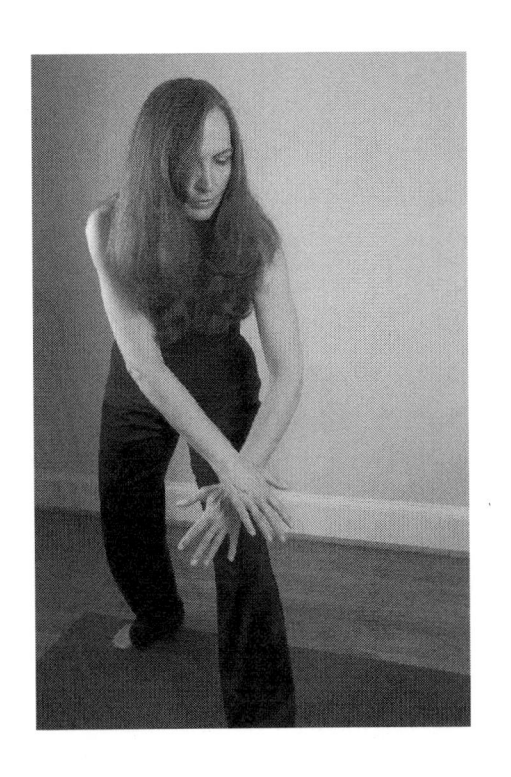

Movement 12

Move the Wave

Arms begin on either side of the left leg. Float the arms up and lean back, and lift the toes of left foot off the floor. Push hands forward lowering toes and hands down to the starting position.

Repeat on the other side.

Movement 13

Flying Dove Spreads Wings

Arms begin on either side of the left leg. Open the arms out to the side, shift the weight to the back leg and lift the toes of the left foot off the floor.

Repeat on the other side.

Movement 14

Push Fist and Stretch the Arm

From Wide Horse Stance, bring the fists to the hips. Bend the knees and punch the left arm forward. Straighten the knees slightly and bring the fist back to the hip. Alternate punching the arms.

Movement 15

Fly Like an Eagle

From Wide Horse Stance, simultaneously straighten the knees slightly and float the arms up and out to the side to shoulder level. Keep the elbows and wrists bent and relaxed. Bend the knees and float the arms down.

Movement 16

Revolve Like a Windmill

Begin with Fly Like an Eagle but continue until the arms are overhead. Bend to the left. Circle down to a forward bend. Continue circling around coming up on the right side. Circle back to the left.

MOVEMENT 17

Play with a Ball Like a Child

Start in Horse Stance. Lift the right leg keeping the knee bent. Simultaneously, raise the left arm. Lower the hand and foot down.

Repeat with the opposite leg and arm.

Movement 18

Quieting the Qi

Start with the hands next to the body in Horse Stance. Turning the palms up, slightly straighten the knees while lifting the arms out to the side and keep the elbows bent. Bring the hands to shoulder height. Turn the palms down, bending the knees, and pushing the hands down.

8 Pieces of Brocade

The movements are done in sequence.

Movement 1

Palms Raised to Heaven

Clasp the hands in front with the palms facing inward. Raise the arms. When the hands are at heart level, turn the hands so the palms face upward and lift the heels. Continue raising the arms until they are overhead. Simultaneously, lower the heels and bring the arms down keeping the hands clasped.

Movement 2

Drawing the Bow

Start in Wide Horse Stance. Lift the hands as if holding a bow. The index finger and thumb of the left hand are in an L-shape; the other fingers are curled at the middle knuckle. Simultaneously bend the knees, and pull the bow back with the right hand. Bring the right hand back to the heart and straighten knees to the starting position.

Repeat on the other side.

Movement 3

Separating Heaven and Earth

Start in Horse Stance. With the hands at heart level, turn the left palm to the ceiling and the right palm to the floor placing the right hand next to the right hip. Lower the hands. As they pass each other, switch and raise the right palm to the ceiling and lower the left hand to hip level with the palm facing downward. Alternate lifting and lowering the hands.

Movement 4

Wise Owl Gazes Back

Stand upright with the feet close together. Turn the head or torso to look behind.

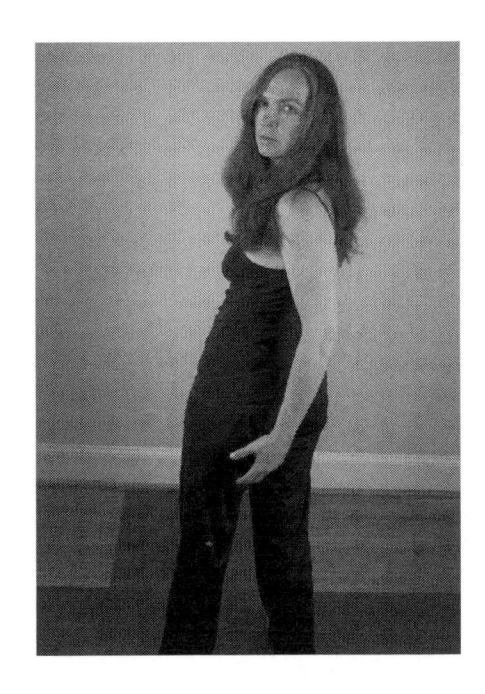

Movement 5
Wag the Dog's Tail

From Wide Horse Stance, place the hands on the knees. Sweep the head and torso to the left, turning the head to the left as the right hip moves to the right. The right leg slightly straightens. Return to center and continue sweeping head and torso to the right. Alternate sweeping side-to-side.

Movement 6
Press the Earth, Touch the Sky

Begin as you would in Palms Raised to Heaven. With the knees slightly bent, fold forward bringing the palms toward the floor. Lift up and arch back.

Movement 7

Punch with Angry Eyes

This movement is the same as Punch Fist and Stretch Arm except that when punching, open eyes wide.

Movement 8

Lift the Heels

Lift the heels and forcibly drop the heels.

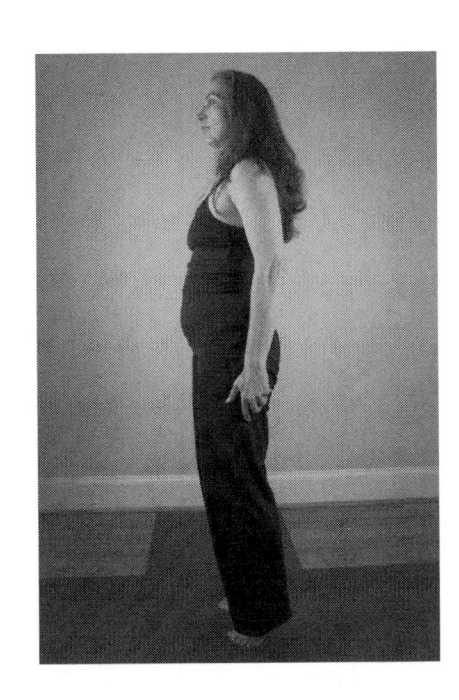

Gather Qi

Front of the Body
Step 1
Begin in Horse Stance. Float the arms up drawing the hands toward the chest. Begin to straighten the arms, leaving the elbows slightly bent with the palms facing outward.

Front of the Body
Step 2
Simultaneously straighten the knees slightly and turn the palms down. Pull the hands toward the body.

Side of the Body

Step 1
Begin in Horse Stance. Float the arms out to the side at shoulder level. Begin to straighten the arms, leaving the elbows slightly bent with the palms facing outward.

Side of the Body

Step 2
Straighten the knees slightly as the palms turn down. Pull the hands toward the body.

Back of the Body

Lift the heels and turn the palms to the back. Pump the hands back as the heels raise and lower.

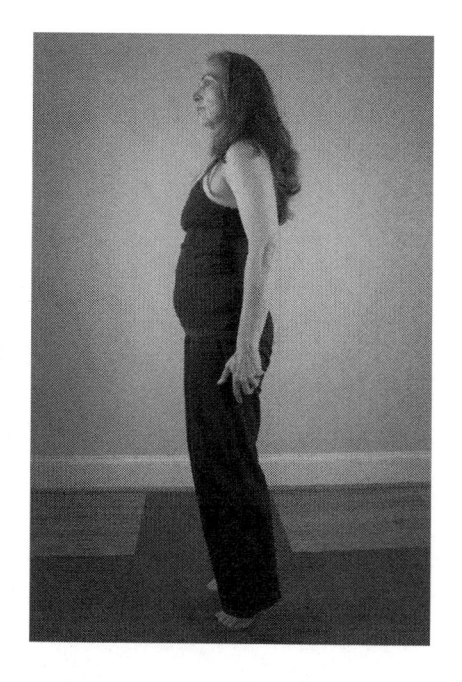

Gather Qi from Heaven

Begin in Horse Stance. Float the arms up bending the elbows. Hands are above the head with the palms down and fingers facing each other.

Gather Qi from the Earth

From Gather Qi from Heaven, clasp hands and turn the palms upward. Fold forward ending with the palms facing down.

Tai Chi Solo Forms

Brush Knee Push Chi

Embrace the Moon with the right hand on top. Turn to the left pushing the right arm to the left and pulling the left hand to the left hip with the palm facing down ending in Bow Stance.

Repeat on the other side starting with the left hand on the top in Embrace the Moon.

Embrace the Moon

Place the hands or arms over one another as if holding onto the top and bottom of a ball.

Heaven and Earth

Step 1

From Horse Stance, cup and bring the hands to the heart. Lift the arms up.

Step 2

Simultaneously turn the head to the left as the hands sweep out to the side. Continue lowering the hands and fold forward. Scoop Qi and come back to Step 1.

Repeat Step 2 looking over the right shoulder.

Parting the Wild Horse's Mane

Embrace the Moon with the right hand on top. Simultaneously turn to the left, assuming a Bow Stance while sweeping the hands in the opposite direction. The left elbow is bent and the palm is facing inward while the right hand is at the right hip and the palm facing downward.

Repeat to the other side with the left hand on top.

Push Chi

Start with the elbows bent. The right hand is higher than the left, with the fingers pointing up, and the palm facing outward. The left hand is parallel to the floor with the left palm facing inward. Draw the left hand toward the body and push the right hand away. Switch position of the hands in the opposite direction and repeat.

White Crane Takes Flight

From Horse Stance, straighten the right knee slightly and lift the left leg, with knee bent. Simultaneously, float the arms up to side keeping the elbows and wrists bent and relax. Simultaneously, lower the arms and right leg.

Repeat lifting the right leg.

Part IV

Qi Infused Yoga Practices

Chapter 12

Qi Infused Yoga Practices

Defining Qi Infused Yoga

Qi Infused Yoga is a new and innovative style of yoga that blends the Eastern practices of Qigong, Tai Chi, and yoga into a fluid practice. Qi Infused Yoga focuses on physical movement as well as the movement of energy. Stagnant Qi and blocked prana awaken and begin to flow as the meridians and chakras are gently accessed via the various Qigong movements and yoga postures. This chapter outlines a 30-, 45-, and 60-minute Qi Infused Yoga practices, which add movements and asanas from the previous one.

30-Minute Qi Infused Yoga Practice

Asana or Movement	Repetitions
Mountain	
Heaven and Earth	6–8
Forward Bend, alternate by bending the knees	
Sun Salutation-variation Perform Sun Salutation Steps 1-6. After Downward Facing Dog, gently drop the knees to the mat and lower the chest to the mat. Walk the hands to the knees. Sit on the Heels Uncurl the toes and lift the knees to stretch the top of the ankles and feet. Downward Facing Dog Perform Sun Salutation Steps 7-9. Repeat Sun Salutation-variation leading with the left foot for Steps 3 and 7.	
Qigong 18 Movements	1
Parting the Wild Horse's Mane	3 each side

30-Minute Qi Infused Yoga Practice

Asana or Movement	Repetitions
Perform asanas on the right side • Warrior II • Reverse Warrior • Triangle • Lunge	1
Straddled Forward Bend	
Perform asanas on the left side • Lunge • Triangle • Warrior II • Reverse Warrior	
Mountain	
Forward Bend	1
Bound Angle Pose	
Head-to-Knee Pose	Both sides
Apanasana	
Corpse	

45-Minute Qi Infused Yoga Practice

Asana or Movement	Repetitions
Mountain	
Heaven and Earth	6–8
Forward Bend, alternate by bending the knees	
Sun Salutation-variation Perform Sun Salutation Steps 1-6. After Downward Facing Dog, gently drop the knees to the mat and lower the chest to the mat. Walk the hands to the knees. Sit on the Heels Uncurl the toes and lift the knees to stretch the top of the ankles and feet. Downward Facing Dog Perform Sun Salutation Steps 7-9. Repeat Sun Salutation-variation leading with the left foot for Steps 3 and 7.	
Roll-down and roll-up • Center • Right • Left Similar to a forward bend, perform the Roll-down by lifting the arms keeping the wrists and elbows slightly bent. Bend the knees and unstack the vertebrae one at a time. Hang like a rag-doll. Perform the Roll-up in the opposite manner stacking the vertebrae one at time.	
Palm-Tree Series Perform Step 5 only	3

45-Minute Qi Infused Yoga Practice

Asana or Movement	Repetitions
Qigong 18 Movements	3
Parting the Wild Horse's Mane	3 each side, alternating
Brush Knee Push Chi	3 each side, alternating
Perform asanas on the right side • Warrior II • Reverse Warrior • Triangle • Lunge Straddled Forward Bend **Perform asanas on the left side** • Lunge • Triangle • Warrior II • Reverse Warrior	1
8 Pieces of Brocade	8
Mountain	
Forward Bend	1
Bound Angle Pose	
Head-to-Knee Pose	Both sides
Apanasana	
Corpse	

60-Minute Qi Infused Yoga Practice

Asana or Movement	Repetitions
Mountain	
Heaven and Earth	6–8
Forward Bend, alternate by bending the knees	
Sun Salutation-variation Perform Sun Salutation Steps 1-6. After Downward Facing Dog, gently drop the knees to the mat. Walk the hands to the knees. Sit on the Heels Uncurl the toes and lift the knees to stretch the top of the ankles and feet. Downward Facing Dog Perform Sun Salutation Steps 7-9. Repeat Sun Salutation-variation leading with the left foot for Steps 3 and 7.	
Sun Salutation-variation Perform Sun Salutation Steps 1-6. After Downward Facing Dog, gently drop the knees to the mat and perform Cat Stretches Sit on the Heels Downward Facing Dog Perform Sun Salutation Steps 7-9. Repeat Sun Salutation-variation leading with the left foot for Steps 3 and 7.	8 each side

60-Minute Qi Infused Yoga Practice

Asana or Movement	Repetitions
Roll-down and roll-up • Center • Right • Left Similar to a forward bend, perform the Roll-down by lifting the arms keeping the wrists and elbows slightly bent. Bend the knees and unstack the vertebrae one at a time. Hang like a rag-doll. Perform the Roll-up in the opposite manner stacking the vertebrae one at time.	3
Palm-Tree Series Perform Step 5 only	3
Gather Qi	6 each direction (front, side, back, top, bottom)
Qigong 18 Movements	1
Parting the Wild Horse's Mane	3 each side, alternating
Brush Knee Push Chi	3 each side, alternating
Goddess Pose	

60-Minute Qi Infused Yoga Practice

Asana or Movement	Repetitions
Perform asanas on the right side	
• Warrior II	
• Reverse Warrior	
• Triangle	
• Side-Angle Bend	
• Lunge	
Straddled Forward Bend	
Straddled Forward Bend (1/2 way up with arms out to side)	
Goddess Pose	
Perform asanas on the left side	
• Warrior II	
• Reverse Warrior	
• Triangle	
• Side-Angle Bend	
• Lunge	
Push Chi	8
Awaken Qi	3
Fly Like an Eagle	3
Perform White Crane Takes Flight lifting left leg	3
Eagle	
Note: Perform Eagle crossing left leg over the right and crossing the right arm over the left	
Repeat series with right leg and left arm	

60-Minute Qi Infused Yoga Practice

Asana or Movement	Repetitions
8 Pieces of Brocade	8
Mountain	
Lunge twist	Both sides
Child's Pose	
Bound Angle Pose	

Cow's Head Pose
 Half Lord of Fishes Pose
     Note: cross right foot over the left leg
 Half Lord of Fishes Pose variation
     Note: straighten left leg
 Head-to-Knee Pose
     Note: Place right foot on the inside of the left thigh
 Repeat all poses with opposite leg and foot	

Apanasana	
Corpse	

Glossary

Acupressure	Apply pressure to specific marma points or points along the meridian
Acupuncture	Insertion of needles at specific points along the meridian
Anandamaya Kosha	The fifth and smallest kosha; also known as the bliss or spirit body
Annamaya Kosha	The first and largest kosha; associated with the physical body
Apana	One of the five major vayus; associated with elimination of bodily fluids
Asana	Yoga pose
Ashtanga	On athletic style of hatha yoga that consists of six series
Ayruveda	Approximately 5,000 year old scientific and holistic medical science
Bandha	Lock or seal
Chakras	Spinning wheels of energy
Chi	Alternate spelling of Qi
Crown Chakra	Wheel of energy located at the top of the head; associated with the color purple
Dosha	Refers to the one of the three (vata, pitta, kapha) possible physical and mental constitutions and the energy associated with the constitution
Five Elements/ Five Element Theory	Theory that all material is made up five elements
Guna	Three principle energies that affect all life
Heart Chakra	Wheel of energy located in the chest at the heart; associated with the color green
Ida	One of the three primary energy channels in the chakra system that starts on the left side and wraps around the sushumna; deals with cooling and passive aspects of the body

Glossary

Iyengar Yoga   Methodical style of yoga developed by B.K.S. Iyengar

Kapha   The dosha associated with the earth and water elements; associated with physical structure of the body

Ki   Japanese term for the life force of all living things

Kundalini   Stored energy

Mana   Hawaiian term for the life force of all living things

Manaomaya Kosha   The third kosha; associated with the mental state and emotions

Marma Point   Specific points on the body that when pressure is applied affect the chakras, doshas, and physical health

Mudra   Creates a seal so energy flows in a closed circuit

Nadis   Energy path ways that often correspond to the physical nerve network

Patañjali   Sage/guru/seer who is credited for creating the yoga sutras

Pingala   One of the three primary energy channels in the chakra system that starts on the right and wraps around the sushumna; deals with heating and active aspects of the body

Pitta   The dosha associated with the fire and water elements; associated with physical, mental, and emotional digestion

Prana   Indian term for the life-force of all living things

Prana Vayu   One of the five major vayus; associated with the chest, throat, mind, heart, sense organs, intelligence, and psychological activities

Pranamaya Kosha   The second kosha; also known as the subtle or energetic body

Glossary

Pranayama	Breathing exercises that direct the flow of prana and awaken kundalini
Qi	Chinese term for the life-force of all living things
Qi Infused Yoga	Style of yoga introduced and explained in this book that combines Qigong, Tai Chi, and yoga asanas in a vinyasa-type practice.
Qigong	A series of movements developed by the Chinese that strengthen and cultivate Qi
Rajas	The guna related to agitation and activation
Reflexology	A specialized massage, generally on the soles of the feet
Root Chakra	Wheel of energy located at the base of the spine; associated with the color red
Sacral Chakra	Wheel of energy located in the lower abdomen; associated with the color orange
Samana	One of the five major vayus; associated with digestion and one's internal fire
Sattva	The guna related to balance
Solar Plexus Chakra	Wheel of energy located at the solar plexus/navel area; associated with the color yellow
Sushumna	One of the three primary energy channels in the chakra system that is located in the center and corresponds to the anatomical spinal column
TCM	Acronym for Traditional Chinese Medicine
Tai Chi	A martial arts application of Qigong
Tamas	The guna related to slowness and lethargy
Third-eye Chakra	Wheel of energy located between the brows; associated with the color indigo
Throat Chakra	Wheel of energy located in the throat; associated with the color blue

Glossary

Udana	One of the five major vayus; associated with regeneration and rejuvenation
Vata	The dosha associated with the air and space element; associated with all movement
Vayus	Associated with movement and air; channels in which prana moves
Vijnanamaya Kosha	The fourth kosha; also known as witness or wisdom body
Vinyasa	Flowing style of yoga where movement is linked with the breath
Vyana	One of the five major vayus; associated with physical movement
Yoga Sutras	196 short statements that are the foundation of yogic philosophy

Citations

1. Keller, Doug. *Refining the Breath*. 2005.
2. Lui, Quingshan. *Chinese Fitness – A Mind/Body Approach*. Boston: YMAA Publication Center. 1997.
3. Allnurses.com. Holistic Nursing. Web. 26 March 2012.

Bibliography

Ashley-Farrand, Thomas. *Healing Mantras*. Saraswati Publications LLC., 17 March 2012.

"Ayurvedic Medicines Kerala India." Naturesmagics Kerala India Tourism Portal. Web. 27 July 2012.

"Buddhism: An Introduction" *Thailand: Jewel of the Orient.* (video) PBS. 17 March 2012.

Chopra, Deepak. *Journey Into Healing-Awakening the Wisdom Within You*. United States: Harmony Books. 1994.

"In 2011 The Baby Boomers Start To Turn 65." End of the American Dream. WordPress. 2012. 6 April 2012

Jarmey, Chris. *The Theory and Practice of Taiji Qigong*. Berkeley: Lotus Publishing. 2003.

Jayaram V. "The Triple Gunas, Sattva, Rajas and Tamas." Hinduwebsite 2012. Web. 12 March 2012.

Johari, Seema. "The 3 Gunas." Sanatan Society 2012. Web. 12 March 2012.

Keller, Doug. "Breath Vayus and Chakras." Do Yoga. pdf. 2007. 14 March 2012.

LaPage, Joseph. *Professional Yoga Therapist Manual*. 2007.

Marchand, Peter. "Ayurvedic Massage Techniques." Sanatan Society 2012. Web. 29 March 2012.

Press, Eileen. *Ayurveda – The Light of Understanding*. 2010.

Reed, Michael. *Acu-Yoga – Designed to Relieve Stress and Tension*. Tokyo: Gach, Japan Publications, Inc. 1981.

Richards, Rick. "What are the Chakras?" Web. 16 March 2012

Sagar, Narayan Vete. "Marma Massage" Ayruveda: The Science of Life. 29 March 2012.

"What are Heaty and Cooling Foods?" Benefits of Honey, 2006-2012. 21 March 2012.

Yang, Jwing-Ming. "Basic Concepts of Qi and Qigong - Part 1." 2009. YMAA. Web. 17 March 2012.

Yarema, Thomas, D. Rhoda and J. Brannigan. "The Five Elements; The Outside is Inside All of Us." in *Eat • Taste • Heal: An Ayurvedic Guidebook and Cookbook for Modern Living*. Five Elements Press 2011. Web. 15 March 2012.

Made in the USA
Charleston, SC
20 January 2014